Midwives
to Nazism

Midwives
to Nazism

University Professors
in Weimar Germany
1925–1933

Alice Gallin

MERCER

ISBN 0-86554-202-3

The paper used in this publication meets the minimum requirements
of American National Standard for Information Sciences—
Permanence of Paper for Printed Library Materials, ANSI Z39.48-1984.

Library of Congress Cataloging-in-Publication Data
Gallin, Alice.
Midwives to Nazism.
Bibliography: p. 115.
Includes index.
1. Universities and colleges—Germany—Faculty—
Attitudes—History—20th century. 2. College teachers—
Germany—Political activity—History—20th century.
3. Germany—Politics and government—1918-1933.
4. Nationalism and education—Germany—History—20th
century. 5. National socialism and education—History—
20th century. I. Title.
LA727.G34   1986   370′.943   86-8792
ISBN 0-86554-202-3 (alk. paper)

Contents

To
my parents and teachers
who gave me my love
for learning and teaching

Acknowledgments

I am deeply grateful to my Ursuline community and the College of New Rochelle for the sabbatical year that enabled me to do the research for this book. In the summer of 1971 I had the opportunity of speaking with Dr. Fritz Ringer, then at MIT, about his work on the German professors, *The Decline of the German Mandarins*. This conversation was the springboard for my own research and writing, so I am therefore indebted to Dr. Ringer in a special way.

Personal appreciation is also due to the Ursulines of Munich and Landshut and to the Theilacker and Messmer families in Stuttgart for their warm hospitality during my stay in Germany. Personnel at the libraries and archives in Munich, Heidelberg, and Tübingen were gracious in their assistance. As on so many other occasions, I benefited from the help and interest of the curators at the National Archives in Washington, D.C.

While I was writing the early drafts of the manuscript, I was supported by the interest and criticism of such friends as Bill and Hincmar, Gerald and Toby, Bridget, Nancy, and Tish. As the project moved along my zeal was maintained by Peggy, Margaret, Amadeus, and Jackie at home, and in the office by David Johnson, my associate director at the Association of Catholic Colleges and Universities. In 1985 the association granted me a three-month leave in order to put the manuscript into final form. All of my colleagues at the National Catholic Education Association and in the various Higher Education Associations have encouraged me and insisted on the importance of the task I undertook. To them I express my thanks.

Above all, I owe an enormous debt of gratitude to Barbara Spies, who read and reread what I wrote and rewrote. Her editorial skills and, even more, her long-standing friendship made the deed possible. Mercer University Press was approached because of the encouragement of Dr. Ben Fisher, former educational director of the Southern Baptist Convention, and his wife Sally—two very dear friends. I thank the staff of the Press for carrying out the editorial work with graciousness and high competence. Clearly, the manuscript would never have reached the publisher without the diligence and perseverance of my administrative assistant, LaVerne McKan-Jones. Dr. John Zeender, professor of history at The Catholic University of America, read an early draft of the book and offered many helpful suggestions.

Needless to say, what is presented here is solely my responsibility. Clio inspired me; Fritz Ringer's work on *The Decline of the German Mandarins* was my starting point. I hope that what I have written will be of value to the academic community within which I have spent many happy years.

Introduction

One bitterly cold afternoon in January 1972 I found myself interviewing Albert Speer in the living room of his charming family home in Heidelberg. Below us was the picturesque medieval university that has been the subject of so much romantic song and story. His wife and grandchildren came in and out as I was served coffee by the side of the large fireplace. A St. Bernard dog arrived to complete the picture of German familial peace.

My purpose in coming to visit with Speer two years after his memoirs had been published in English[1] was to find out if he connected the life he had led with the education he had received. What did he remember about the climate of the universities in his student days? Could he confirm any of the hypotheses with which I was beginning my work on the role of the Weimar professors in preparing the way for Hitler?

As we talked he did indeed confirm several of my assumptions:[2] 1) that the professors, in general, ignored the need to prepare students for participation in the political life of the Republic; 2) that the majority of them were averse to any change, whether inside or outside the university; 3) that a "traditional" anti-Semitism existed among both professors and students; and 4) that the high degree of specialization in the curricula precluded interdisciplinary studies, which might have brought about some integration of classical studies and contemporary issues. He spoke of his delight that the students now were receiving "political education," by which he meant that they were being urged to reflect on and write about contemporary questions. He contrasted this new mode of education with his own experience; politics had never been discussed at home or in school, nor with his fellow students at the Technical Institutes he attended in Munich and Berlin.

---

[1]Albert Speer, *Inside the Third Reich: Memoirs by Albert Speer* (New York: The Macmillan Company, 1970).

[2]The interview took place in Heidelberg on 17 January 1972. It is recorded on a tape in the possession of the author.

In his memoirs Speer had expressed some surprise that his father did not speak to him of political matters, especially because he was a "liberal" even before 1914, in that he was a follower of Friedrich Naumann and read the daily *Frankfurter Zeitung*. However, he admits that had his father embarked on such a conversation he would have "dodged" it.[3] His only concern, as best he could recall it after reading through all the letters he had sent to his fiancée when he was studying, was to finish his architectural studies and get married. Politics in the years 1924-1930 held no interest for him.

When engaged in writing *Inside the Third Reich*, Speer consciously tackled the question of his own role in Hitler's regime. Intermittently throughout the book he raises questions about how much he knew of the designs of Hitler in both domestic and foreign policies and how great his responsibility was. It struck me that in 1972 he had not yet found satisfactory answers to his questions.

This distinguished-looking man in his mid-sixties, released in 1966 after serving a twenty-year term in Spandau, showed no effects of such incarceration. He was alert, gracious, thoughtful, and quite willing to listen to my questions and to reflect with me on his experience. Yet, as we spoke, the more puzzled I became and the less I felt that I understood him. There was such a lack of clarity in his evaluation of moral responsibility—his own and others'—that I wondered at his apparent peace.

His reference in his memoirs to the fact that he had "compartmentalized" his mind may be the key.[4] As late as 1944 he sent a memo to Hitler in which he stated: "The task I have to fulfill is an unpolitical one." He also saw that his "habit of thinking within the limits of my own field provided me, both as an architect and as Armaments Minister, with many opportunities for evasion." Yet, he finally judged himself: "But in the last analysis, I myself determined the degree of my isolation, the extremity of my evasions, and the extent of my ignorance."[5]

He spoke to me of an anti-Semitism in the universities that was a "given" among families of his social status; he thought that about eighty percent of his fellow students were from the well-to-do (but not "wealthy") class. Yet he insisted it was not like the anti-Semitism of Hitler. He recalled that in Berlin the Jewish students in architecture tended to go into the seminars led by "leftist" professors. He felt that they were never quite accepted by other students either in Munich or in Berlin.

---

[3] Speer, *Inside the Third Reich*, 8.

[4] Ibid., 112.

[5] Ibid., 113.

This general climate of anti-Semitism may explain how he could have written, "Hitler's hatred of the Jews seemed to me so much a matter of course that I gave it no serious thought."[6] Speer himself has not been seen by historians of the period as anti-Semitic, yet he later recognized that his "non-questions" about the operations of the concentration camps constituted, at the very least, a sin of omission. At Nuremberg he said that he took "full responsibility . . . for the crimes committed, for the slave labor in the factories under his authority, for his collaboration with the SS when it provided concentration camp prisoners for his production lines, and his conspicuous role in a regime that killed—although with no direct help from him—six million Jews."[7] Was he so inured to the anti-Semitic climate of German life that he could ignore what was happening?

It was in 1931 that Speer became a member of the National Socialist party in Berlin. He was, at the time, an assistant to his former professor, Heinrich Tessenow, and attended a meeting of university students and teachers addressed by Adolf Hitler. Tessenow and several of his liberal colleagues had often been the target of Nazi attacks, and yet Speer could overlook that in his enthusiasm for the new movement once he heard Hitler speak. He points out that he did not tell Tessenow of his decision to join the party at that time.[8]

Speer attributes this crucial decision to join the party to the inadequacy of his own education.[9] Both at home and in school, he claims, he had not received the tools he needed to argue with the very talented and articulate National Socialist students he was now instructing for Tessenow. He and other young people were very depressed by the political weakness and economic inadequacy of the Weimar government; and without really studying the writings and platform of the Nazis, he responded to the enthusiasm he witnessed among them. In speaking with me, Speer used the analogy of infection in the human body: "If there are no antibodies within the body, infection enters and meets with no resistance." In his opinion, this is what happened to the young people of his generation, and he blames his unpreparedness and theirs on a faulty education.

Is this a valid judgment? Speer had brought me back to my original question and phrased it a new way: "Why did the professors in the German universities fail in the task of helping their students develop the needed antibodies?" Was it fair to expect them to have done so? Should they have provided the German people with a model of resistance rather than one of compliance?

---

[6]Ibid., 112.

[7]Eugene Davidson, Introduction to Speer, *Inside the Third Reich*, xiii.

[8]Speer, *Inside the Third Reich*, 18.

[9]Ibid., 19. This was confirmed by several of his remarks in the interview.

An earlier work of mine, *The German Resistance to Hitler: Ethical and Religious Factors*,[10] had introduced me to various groups of Germans who had resisted Hitler. While not all of them were willing to go as far as tyrannicide with the conspirators of 20 July 1944, in their own ways they offered consistent resistance to unjust laws and found ways of circumventing government regulations that they considered unethical or immoral. I found cells of resistance in the army, the intelligence circles, the labor unions, and the churches, but none in the universities. The notable exception was the small group in Munich known as the Scholl group, made up of students and one professor, Kurt Huber. All were put to death for the publication of anti-Hitler pamphlets in February 1943. No protest was registered by the university for this outrage.

In the early 1970s we in the United States experienced our own moment of truth in the universities. The sudden tragedy at Kent State, in response to the unauthorized bombing of Cambodia, provoked demonstrations on many campuses throughout the nation. Faculties and students alike debated the role of their universities in political decision making. Arguments for and against "taking a stand" as an institution were often raucous and prolonged. Those in favor of a public position being taken against the war in Vietnam insisted that the university had a sacred duty to be a critic of society, and that not to take a stand would be as political as to do so. On the other side, many argued that a university would lose its own special character as guardian of academic freedom if it ventured, as an institution, into the political arena. Proponents of both these contradictory positions often argued from "the German experience." Some claimed that had the professors in Germany been more politically involved, they would have played a significant role in keeping Hitler from coming to power. If they had missed that chance, one might hope that they would have participated in the resistance activities designed to overthrow him. As critics of society and defenders of humanistic values, the professors had a duty to fight Nazism from the very beginning. On the other hand, those who favored the position that the university should remain outside of the political arena insisted that it was when the university became "politicized" by the pro-Nazi students and junior faculty that the real disaster occurred. To them, the professors should have remained "above politics," going about their own business and ignoring the political scene.

Curiosity, then, about the "German experience" of academia and its relation to politics impelled me to undertake this study. Satisfied from the evi-

---

[10]Mary Alice Gallin, O.S.U., *The German Resistance to Hitler: Ethical and Religious Factors* (Washington: The Catholic University of America Press, 1955).

dence that the professors had not been part of the active resistance forces,[11] I wondered why. Was there something about the nature of a university that inhibited them? Was there a conscious philosophy behind their refusal to participate in the democratic form of government? Did the advent of National Socialism take them by surprise? As defenders of an educational tradition that centered on *Bildung* (the concept of a truly humanistic formation), how could they have ignored the social dimension of intellectual development? The basic question for me was: How were academia and politics related in the pre-Hitler period of German history?

Because the institutional aspect of the university's role in society was critical to my own experience in the 1970s, I decided to limit my study to the role of the faculty. Decisions about taking a stand vis-à-vis governmental policies were undoubtedly influenced by students—in both Weimar Germany and in the United States in the 1970s—but the ultimate call for university action had to come from the faculties or it did not come at all. Actually, more has been written about the growth of the radical Right among students in the German universities than about the political persuasions of their professors. The way in which conservative students paved the way for the National Socialist intrusion into academia has been well described.[12]

Since I am concerned primarily about the impact of the faculty on the university's public role, I have also limited my inquiry to full professors, those who constituted the "Small Senates" that were the locus of power at the time. I have further set parameters on my study geographically and chronologically. The years 1925-1933 were chosen because the coalition governments of that time allowed for active participation by the professors whether they came from the Left or the Right, and the economic stability Germany was then enjoying should have lowered the level of anxiety about communism.[13]

---

[11]The absence of professors in the various circles of resistance is clear not only from my own work but also in later publications. Cf. Peter Hoffman, *The History of the German Resistance, 1933-1945* (Cambridge MA: MIT Press, 1977): Harold C. Deutsch, *The Conspiracy against Hitler* (Minneapolis: The University of Minnesota Press, 1968); Ernst Christian Helmreich, *The German Churches under Hitler* (Detroit: Wayne State University Press, 1979).

[12]One of the most helpful works in English on the role of students is: Michael Stephen Steinberg, *Sabers and Brown Shirts* (Chicago: The University of Chicago Press, 1977). See also Konrad H. Jarausch, *Students, Society and Politics in Imperial Germany* (Princeton: Princeton University Press, 1982) for a good historical background to the Weimar period.

[13]This distinction between 1918-1923 and 1924-1933 is supported by Walter H.

Second, I have focused on the universities of Bavaria and Württemburg because it was in those *Lände* that conservative monarchists might have found a way to cooperate with the Center party and thus have joined battle with the National Socialists at the beginning of the movement, thereby forestalling its eventual triumph. The shift of some leaders of the German Democratic party (DDP) and the German National People's party (DNVP) toward support of the Weimar Republic (for reasons of the head rather than of the heart) was, with very few exceptions, not reflected in the professorial ranks. By their stubborn adherence to a nonpolitical image of themselves, the majority of the professors missed the opportunity to work with the moderate forces and unfortunately, albeit unintentionally, allowed the extreme Rightists to coalesce and thus determine Germany's future.

It is my contention that by such a refusal the professors let themselves become midwives to National Socialism.[14] The use of such a term, as is the case with all analogical language, is not without its difficulties. Some students of the period prefer the term "passive observers" or "unpolitical bystanders," yet I find that a stronger term is necessary.

The midwife is one who facilitates the birth of the child—the one who, by her presence, assists the parents at the critical moment a child is brought into the world. We do not hold the midwife accountable for the conception and pregnancy; nor do we consider her responsible for the way the child turns out in later life. Her contribution is made at a particular and critical moment. The skills that she has developed through education and experience serve the needs of the parents.

Like the midwife, the professors of Weimar brought their skills to society, skills that came from their own particular education and experience. While not intending to do so (and in this they are unlike the midwife), they opened the minds and hearts of their students to currents of nationalism and romanticism and thus made them receptive to the rhetoric and charisma of Hitler. The environment created by them within the universities, far from being one that engendered critics of authoritarianism and traditionalism, promoted conformity, passivity, and a distaste for political action. They thought that they were men-

---

Kaufmann, *Monarchism in the Weimar Republic* (New York: Bookman Associates, 1953). He writes: "[Whereas the years 1918-1923] stood under the sign of disorder and unrest, the period since 1924 was favorably characterized by stabilization of the political situation in Germany, by *rapprochement* with the victorious nations and by a moderate economic prosperity" (117).

[14]I first came across the use of the term *midwives* to describe the professors of Weimar in Hans Peter Bleuel, *Deutschlands Bekenner Professoren zwischen Kaiserreich und Diktatur* (München: Scherz, 1968) 8.

tors of society, "above politics" as they described it, and thus absolved from political responsibility. Given completely to research and teaching in highly specialized fields, the professors forgot the broader purpose of the university: the development of persons capable of and committed to the building of a more humane society.

It is the purpose of this book to examine three ways in which the professors made it easy for those who brought the Third Reich to birth. The first was by their refusal to accept political responsibility within the Weimar Republic; that is, they claimed to be "unpolitical" while being strongly German Nationalist. Second, they uncritically promoted a mode of speaking that glorified the so-called German virtues, denounced parliamentary democracy, and invoked visions of future German glory. Finally, within the university itself—which can be seen as a microcosm of society at large—they clung to a rigid structure of elitist government and a curriculum that demonstrated little relevance to the interests and needs of the students. Their stated goal of *Bildung*—the education that would lead to the cultivated person—was surrendered to a sterile professionalism.

Their role at this critical juncture was active as well as passive, facilitating rather than obstructionist, and encouraged—if only by silence—the forces in Germany that were moving ever further to the Right.

Chapter One

Politics and the "Unpolitical" Professors

In the spring of 1926 a handful of professors issued an invitation to their colleagues to attend a meeting in Weimar 23-24 April. The announcement began with an admission that the professors had, on the whole, been playing a very negative role in the political life of the nation.

> All too strong among the university professors have been the voices of mistrust and the negative attitude toward the new order in our civil life. All too great has been their effect on the spirit of the students and their influence in turning the honorable and strong national will into unhealthy, yes even perverted, channels.

It was a call to assume at last "the responsibility which we, not only as learned men but also as teachers and educators, have toward our people and their future . . . to rise to the demands of the moment with the greatest energy as soon as it is possible."[1]

Friedrich Meinecke, professor of history at the University of Berlin and later dean of German historians, was the chief architect of this meeting. He had been a collaborator with Ernest Troeltsch and Adolf von Harnack in the formation of the Popular League for Freedom, organized in 1917, and had also worked to found the German Democratic party (DDP) the following year. Although he did not remain active in the party ranks for very long—perhaps due to the deaths of his two collaborators, Max Weber and Friedrich Naumann—he did remain a *Vernunftrepublikaner*, someone who was a "Republican of the Head."

Meinecke had recognized in 1919 that "if a man cannot have what he loves then he must love what he has."[2] Hence he admitted that while his heart would

---

[1]Wilhelm Kahl, Friedrich Meinecke, and Gustav Radbruch, *Die deutschen Universitäten und der heutige Staat* (Tübingen: C. B. Mohr, 1926) 3.

[2]Friedrich Meinecke, *Nach der Revolution: Geschichtliche Betrachtugen über unsere Lage* (München: Oldenbourg, 1919) 117.

always cling to the ideal of a monarchy, he knew that such an ideal had been shattered and that at the present moment in history the Weimar Republic and its constitution were the best means of promoting the life of the nation. In 1926[3] he urged his colleagues not to destroy Germany by their steadfast refusal to accept the Republic but rather to "build a bridge over the unhappy cleavage which has developed in the nation through world war and revolution and to win over the German universities and technical institutes whose spirit can never be indifferent to public life."[4] He admitted his own predilection for the monarchy in words with which they could surely empathize:

> Our opponents of yesterday are still for the most part our opponents of today, and today's tension has grown out of the historical tension of yesterday. We are no longer fighting about war aims, but we are fighting over the question of whether the old political world of Germany, which was allured into defeat through every adventuresome war aim and means of war, deserved to collapse in this historical defeat and whether the new political form which we have created can claim a full historical right to life for itself. . . . Many of us, and I believe most of us, were until 9 November 1918 sincere monarchists and have deplored with the deepest sorrow the demise of the old and honored monarchy and Empire.[5]

But, said Meinecke, "An inflexible necessity, not an ideology nor a doctrinal position, leads us to accept the democratic Republic." Since the government was now headed by the conservative Hindenburg, Meinecke argued, it made little or no sense for the professors to oppose him in the name of conservatism. How can Weimar be accused now of being "Leftist"? Rather, continued Meinecke, it is now "reasonable" for the professors to assume co-responsibility with the government for educating its citizens in the meaning of democracy based on an acknowledgment of each individual's dignity. This, he stressed, would keep their role an "academic" and not a "political" one; their task was to introduce "spiritual aristocracy" into a "political democracy" in order to make it noble. Without becoming involved in politics, they should give of their "spiritual wealth" to the country and thus "pay their taxes."[6]

In the words Meinecke used to communicate his message to his colleagues, one finds firsthand documentary evidence of the professorial mentality that predominated among them. By his inferences he has revealed their rejection of democracy, their fear of the Left, and their refusal to relate the mission of the university to the contemporary political realities.

---

[3]Kahl et al., *Die deutschen Universitäten*, 17-31 for Meinecke's speech.

[4]Ibid., 19.

[5]Ibid., 10-11.

[6]Ibid.

His audience included, unfortunately, only about fifty or sixty professors. It was not clear whether the invitation list had been restricted or whether it was widely distributed but not responded to by many. The co-sponsors of the invitation were: Hans Delbruck, Adolf von Harnack, Heinrich Herkner, Wilhelm Kahl, Gustav Mayer, Walther Nernst, Karl Stählin, and Werner Weisbach, all of the University of Berlin. Using the signatures appended to the final declaration issued at the end of the meeting, one notes that the only ones present from Munich were Walter Lotz and the retired Lujo Brentano. From Tübingen Wilhelm von Blume and Ernst Schuster attended (both identified elsewhere as democrats) and from Heidelberg came Gerhard Anshütz, Graf Alexander von Dohna, Karl Heinsheimer, Willy Hellpach, Emil Lederer, Carl Newmann, Richard Thoma, and Alfred Weber. Since many of these men were associated at one time or another with "democratic" groups, it may have been a matter of the "converted" speaking to themselves at this meeting.

However, the *Berliner Tägeblatt,* itself supportive of the Republic, expressed its pleasure at the fact that the meeting was attended by so many professors from a wide spectrum of political affiliations. A comment in this article confirms a picture of the universities as anti-Weimar: "[The] often-lamented but indisputable fact is that a large part of the rising generation in academic circles are opposed to the new state and cling to a form of the state from an outmoded tradition."[7]

In addition to Meinecke's address to the group, there were two other formal presentations: one by Professor Wilhelm Kahl, a professor of law and a member of the Reichstag for four years, and the other by Professor Gustav Radbruch, an eminent Berlin jurist who became a professor at Heidelberg and later furnished legal counsel for Emil Gumbel.[8] Kahl deplored the fact that so many of his colleagues desired the death of the Republic—in the hope, they said, that out of its ashes a new State would arise—and he urged them to think of the effect that this attitude was having on the students in the universities. Freedom to criticize the constitution and to work towards its amendment did not cancel the fact that the constitution was the center to which their political efforts should be directed. Constructive thinking concerning political action was urged upon the professors as they took up the theme for the meeting: "The Position of the University in the Public Life of the Present Time."

Kahl dwelt on the role played by the professors in 1848, thereby suggesting that the present university community should also be on the side of the democratic reforms. Universities in the past, he said, were considered a source and

---

[7]*Berliner Tägeblatt,* 25 April 1926.

[8]The case of Emil Gumbel is treated in detail in ch. 4.

power for rebirth. It was in them that a place was provided for the members of the society who thought "differently." Kahl saw the events since the end of the war as constitutive of a new world order, not just of a new German nation, and he pointed out that unless Germany worked in full realization of this fact it would have no place at all in that new world order.

The basic disunity that he perceived in the universities rested on divergent views of the Weimar Republic. He begged his colleagues to recognize—and communicate to their students—that it was not the *form* of the State that was important but rather the common "sense of the State" (*Staatsgesinnung*).[9]

A similar plea was made by Radbruch. He deplored the role the professors had been playing, allowing themselves to be the victims of a kind of propaganda when they should in fact be exercising critical judgment befitting their academic status.

> For a long time now the University has been more a conduit than a leader of the spirit of the times. . . . Only too often both before and after the war have the professors sounded the trumpet without knowing for whom or why they were sounding it. . . . With the gestures of leadership, the universities were often the ones led, and they have not been led by the spirit of the times.[10]

Radbruch emphasized the weakness of an educational system in which the children of the working class still represented only 1.3 percent of the student body in the universities. He urged his colleagues to support the Weimar government in its efforts to broaden the base of educational opportunity by uniting the various classes within society. The professors should put their strength and power behind the legal system, for in a democratic Republic the structures are dependent upon the law.

Meinecke then made some very concrete proposals to the group. They, as academically trained leaders of the people, should devote some attention to the fundamental political problems inherent in the new form of government. He suggested a profound study and discussion of such topics as: the office of the president, the problem of minority groups, the goal of a "Great Germany," economic interests, and the themes of democracy and spiritual culture. In short, said Meinecke, the professors should be the "bridge" over the gulf now existing between the old and the new.[11]

These three speeches by Kahl, Meinecke, and Radbruch comprise the printed report of the meeting in Weimar in April 1926. (The report was published that same year.) The call to political responsibility issued by the speak-

---

[9]Kahl et al., *Die deutschen Universitäten*, 10-11.

[10]Ibid., 33.

[11]Ibid., 19.

ers serves as proof that, for the most part, the German professors were antidemocratic and were doing their best to undermine the Republic. A mandate that they work for their country's well-being in this new situation was given to them by a small minority within their own ranks. This was seven years before the Nazi seizure of power. The professors who spoke to the assembly at this meeting feared the disintegration of the German State unless the leaders of the academic community acted to stem the tide. Obviously, they sensed the growing alienation among the youth and recognized the danger of the National Socialist movement among the students.

At the conclusion of the two-day meeting, those who had attended it drew up and signed a statement elucidating the task before them:

> The undersigned university professors have come together in Weimar on the 23 and 24 of April and have spoken together about the task of university professors in public life and have deliberated about the duty which the seriousness of the times places upon them. It is intended to hold such meetings again and to give them the broadest possible scope. Every one of our colleagues is welcome to come who—without prejudice to his fundamental political beliefs—is willing to work together positively in the present democratic-republican state for our present constitution and for the education of the growing generation toward good citizenship in the service of the great German community.[12]

The positive cooperation in the service of the Republic and its constitution envisioned here never saw the light of day. There is no reference to this Weimar meeting and its message of education for good citizenship in any of the archival sources examined. Men who were at the universities in those years have, at best, a very vague recollection of such a gathering. No report seems to have been given by those who attended the meeting to their colleagues in academic senates, nor is the message reflected in the annual rectors' addresses. There is no evidence that the meeting had any impact, and although there was another meeting in 1927 with an attendance double that of the previous year, the gatherings declined each subsequent year until in 1932 only fifteen or twenty came together.[13]

What explains the failure of this attempt on the part of Meinecke and the others to influence the professors, both those that came to the meeting and their colleagues back at the universities? The arguments put forth certainly seem convincing, and the reasonableness of the position taken by the *Vernunftre-publikaners*—namely, that the heart may have its own feelings about the monarchy, but the head saw an "inflexible necessity" (Meinecke) to accept the new State—appears self-evident to the historian.

---

[12]Ibid., conc.

[13]Werner Weisbach, *Geist und Gewalt* (Wien: A. Schroll, 1956) 258-59.

And yet they could not swallow this bitter pill. Why not? Judging from their writings and speeches, many of the professors saw the Weimar Republic as a hiatus in German history, a temporary aberration from the true German State. This was because a "true" state required an affinity with the basic cultural mission (*Kulturmission*) of the German people (*Volk*). A Republic born out of defeat with a base in socialist power could not be open to the richness of this mission. The circumstances surrounding the birth of the Republic had indeed never augured well for its future: military defeat on the Western Front, revolution and mutiny behind the lines, economic devastation, and spiritual despair. It was a sudden and unwanted creation in the wake of World War I and, to them, an *Unrechtsstaat*—one totally inappropriate for the German nation and one to which they could not give allegiance.

Unprepared for defeat, the country was equally unprepared for the Weimar Republic. The delegates of the National Assembly, created in 1919 at a time of chaos, had the unpleasant task of accepting the peace terms at Versailles. They thus received more contempt and opprobrium than the emperor and his officials who had led the nation into war. It was clear that these "unGerman traitors" could not be worthy of affirmation, and much of the academic rhetoric of the 1920s criticizes them sharply for attempting to fulfill the terms of the treaty, for lacking the leadership qualities of a Bismarck, and for accepting the "war guilt lie" about Germany's singular responsibility for the outbreak of hostilities. The university professors picked up from the journalists of the Right the legend of the "stab-in-the-back" as the explanation for Germany's humiliation, and they disseminated this strong nationalistic message to the university students: the true German nation had not been defeated at the Front, but had been undercut by the leftist "criminals" at home.

Hence they would affirm Meinecke's statement of the present reality in 1926: "We are no longer fighting about war aims, but we are fighting over the question of whether the old political world of Germany, which was allured into defeat through every adventuresome war aim and means of war, deserved to collapse in this historical defeat and whether the new political form which we have created can claim a full historical right to life for itself."

But they would strongly deny his exhortation to recognize the right of the Weimar Republic to live. They clearly rejected the Republic and wanted nothing to do with it, least of all to be identified with it. They did not participate in it.

Was this rejection of a political role something new for the professors? Did they have any precedent for involvement in the political life of the nation? Was there a continuity in their self-description as "above politics"?

Only twice in the nineteenth century do we find examples of an active part being played by the academic leaders, one in a very particular academic protest and the other by membership in the Frankfort Assembly of 1848.

In 1837 seven members of the faculty at Göttingen—known later as the "Göttingen Seven"—protested the action of Ernest Augustus, duke of Cumberland, when he ascended the throne of Hanover; he had, according to them, invalidated the constitution. All seven lost their chairs at the university and two were later banished from the kingdom.[14] A decade later (1848) the professors played a key role in the Frankfort Assembly, but the failure of this experiment in democracy led to a fairly widespread withdrawal from the political scene.

With notable exceptions during the struggle for unification, the professors did not emerge into the public political forum again until July 1915 when 352 of them signed the "Intellectuals' Petition."[15] The object of this petition, with a total of 1,347 signatures, was to strengthen German determination to expand territory both at home and abroad. When the war erupted in August 1914, the popular understanding of what was at stake was simply and purely defending the Fatherland against the aggressive actions of Russia, France, and England. By mid-1915, however, the argument had been developed that future security for Germany required it to take the opportunity of extending its geographical limits both in the East and in the West. These annexationists further insisted that she must acquire colonies and spheres of influence in the Far East and Africa, as a competitor with other great powers. Her destiny, to be a world power, mandated living space and greater economic resources. The university professors have been blamed for their leadership in this shift to annexationist goals.

> The most active group of propagandists was composed of university professors, among them chiefly economists and historians. The German professors, as will be remembered, had played a prominent role in the formation of a national sentiment in the age of German unification. Yet, although in the writings and speeches of a good many of them chauvinistic overtones could be discerned, even Heinrich von Trietschke, the least inhibited advocate of power politics of the generation, was still very much aware of the greatness of Europe's multinational tradition which he wished to see preserved. In contrast, the German professors of 1914 had forgotten their obligation to the European cultural tradition and with their appeal to popular vanity and passion tended to disregard their foremost duty, the spread of knowledge.[16]

In terms of political party alignment, the goals of the annexationists were adopted by the Conservatives, the National Liberals, and the Center party. The

---

[14]Karl Dietrich Bracher, *The German Dictatorship* (New York: Praeger, 1970) 16. Translator's note.

[15]Fritz K. Ringer, *The Decline of the German Mandarins* (Cambridge MA: Harvard University Press, 1969) 190.

[16]Hajo Holborn, *A History of Modern Germany, 1840-1945* (New York: Alfred A. Knopf, 1969) 447.

Progressive People's party favored much more limited objectives and the Social Democrats held strongly to the ideal of a purely defensive war.

The professors, many of whom displayed pan-German sympathies, went along with the majority. A group of ninety-three distinguished intellectuals issued a statement defending Germany's preemptive occupation of Belgium. Their instinctive antisocialist, anticommunist, and anti-Jewish sentiments put them in the camp of those who saw Germany as merely defending herself against the dangers from East and West.

The opportunity for a negotiated settlement with the Allies in the summer of 1917 foundered on these same annexationist aims. The Reichstag's Peace Resolution, initiated by the Social Democrats and supported by the Center party, was aborted. Thus the war moved on into 1918, taking more lives and extending the damage and loss of property in many directions.[17]

Wilson's Fourteen Points had been offered in January of 1918. A group of moderates had urged General Ludendorff to accept them, but to no avail. The only two professors named in the group that urged this course of action were Frederick Naumann and Alfred Weber. With the collapse of Russia in March 1918, one might have expected a reversal of fortune on the Western Front, but instead by July of 1918 it seemed clear that the Imperial Armies were facing disaster.[18]

In November 1918 the annexationists had to surrender their grandiose schemes for expansion; they also had to face a crushing and decisive defeat. Germany's inability to realize its imperial longings for world power left a nation disbelieving as well as disappointed. The professors shared in the general disillusionment and retreated, once again, to their studies and classrooms. They contented themselves with the thought that, after all, the mission of the university was a purely "spiritual" one, one they would carry out by preserving German "culture" until the proper instrument for their culture-mission could be forged anew. Their excursion into politics had ended.

It is not surprising, then, that the professors formed a stubborn nucleus of antidemocratic thought in the Weimar era. The State, by definition the foundation of German culture, could not be allowed to depend on the give-and-take of political parties. The professors must remain "above party" and fulfill their role as protectors of the culture. They therefore assumed the task (somehow "unpolitical" in their understanding of it) of fighting against the Republic.

---

[17]Koppel S. Pinson, *Modern Germany* (New York: The Macmillan Company, 1966) 324, 315-16.

[18]Holborn, *A History of Modern Germany*, 500-501.

Thomas Mann touched on this separation of "culture" from "politics" in a talk he gave to the students at the University of Munich in 1923. He explained that the "cultivated" man worked to develop an inwardness—a care for tending the shaping, deepening, and perfecting of one's own personality or, in religious terms, a concern for one's own salvation. This understanding of *Bildung*—the education leading to the "cultivated" person—is subjective and finds the objective world, the world of politics, to be profane. "What I mean by all this," said Mann, "is that the idea of a republic meets with resistance in Germany chiefly because the ordinary middle-class man here, if he ever thought about culture, never considered politics to be part of it, and still does not do so today."[19] Such an understanding of *Bildung* results in an indifference to politics that can be disastrous.[20]

Hugo Preuss, one of the drafters of the Weimar constitution, told the delegates in the Assembly: "How foreign a parliamentary system seems to even the most enlightened Germans."[21] He pleaded with the delegates to help the people overcome their fear of what seemed so alien.

It is important to recognize that it was precisely this perception of the Weimar Republic as "alien" that was at the heart of the professors' opposition. The "cultivated" person was at home in a political environment that promoted the same cultural values traditionally esteemed by the universities: home, church, diligence in study, the arts in their classical form, the nobility of service. Loyalty to the "nation" was a major cultural value, one that transcended at times particular laws of the State. The Republic was experienced as culturally pluralistic. As such, it was contrary to the *Einheit* (unity) of the German *Volk* (people) and a source of divisiveness.

Much of the opposition to the Republic was couched in terms of "un-German" values, namely those of the French Revolution: liberty, equality, fraternity. It was argued that acceptance of "equality" would mean that the German values to which the professors adhered could be revised by majority vote. They considered cultural relativism indigenous to a democratic ideology and contradictory to the German *Kulturmission*. The Republic was therefore unacceptable because it was the fruit of Western political thought; it was not harmonious with the concept of a State arising naturally from a community of the *Volk*.

---

[19]W. H. Bruford, *The German Tradition of Self-Cultivation* (New York: Cambridge University Press, 1975) intro.

[20]Ibid., 207.

[21]Erich Eyck, *A History of the Weimar Republic,* vol. 1 (New York: Atheneum, 1970) 66, quoting Preuss's speech of 8 April 1919.

It was logical for the professors to shun an active role in the political life of the new State. Political parties were seen as channels for diverse philosophies and opposing points of view. More important, they were to be viewed as sources of political power as cabinets succeeded one another depending on party strength or weakness. To Conservatives such as Oswald Spengler, the parties were in conflict with the people. In the Weimar constitution, he complained, "there was no mention of the people, but only of parties, no talk of power, honor or greatness, but only of parties; there was no goal and no future for Germany, but only the interests of parties."[22]

The professors preferred not to participate in such parties. They insisted that they were—and must remain—"above politics." They were the defenders of the "German nation" and must not become embroiled in everyday workings of the governing structures. To them, the concept of the "nation" soared high above that of the State, and their commitment was obviously to the former. Not only did they consider the form of any State as necessarily subservient to the fundamental national "spirit," they also strongly objected to the present State—Weimar—because it was incapable of embodying the values of the nation.

These national values tended to focus on the heroic. One discovers in the 1920s an almost mystical fixation with the tremendous experience of German unity that was engendered by being at the Front (*Fronterlebnis*).[23] As they recalled the year 1914, writers and poets dwelt on the feelings of purposefulness and camaraderie that characterized the German troops as they marched forward in defense of the Fatherland. The call to arms was experienced as a creative and ennobling vocation. Thomas Mann wrote in *The Magic Mountain* of the need for a purgation of Europe from cultural decadence, and he envisioned the descent from the hospital on the mountain top to the plain below, where battle was to be done, as a sign of renewed health and integrity. Even Friedrich Meinecke, despite his conversion to the Republic, recalled 1914 thirty years later in glowing terms:

> The exaltation of the August days of 1914, despite its ephemeral character, is for all who lived through them one of the most precious and unforgettable memories of the highest sort . . . one perceived in all camps that the mere unity of a

---

[22]Kurt Sontheimer, "Anti-Democratic Thought in the Weimar Republic," in *The Road to Dictatorship* (London: Oswald Wolff, 1964) 52.

[23]See the discussion of this phenomenon in Kurt Sontheimer, *Antidemokratisches Denken in der Weimarer Republik* (München: Nymphenburger Verlag, 1962) 122-25 and Christoph Weisz, *Geschichtsauffassung und politisches Denken Münchener Historiker der Weimarer Zeit* (Berlin: Duncker and Humblot, 1970) 151-54.

functional partnership would not suffice, but that a spiritual renovation of our state and culture was necessary.[24]

This idealization of 1914 was particularly important for the generation of university students in the late 1920s because their professors came back to it over and over again. On the day set aside to commemorate the Foundation of the Reich, academic orators often chose as a topic "Langemarck," a reference to the place where brave young German soldiers had marched courageously to their death.

In a speech on 19 November 1926, Professor Oswald Bumke, rector at the University of Munich, spoke glowingly of the German spirit shown by the regiment of university students at Langemarck and concluded: "Go, young Germans, and bring back to us the faith in the pure German soul and in a free German future. Honor our dead fallen in battle and be as they were!"[25]

Almost any topic could serve as an excuse for bringing up the same idea. In an address by a rector chosen from the medical faculty at the University of Munich, Professor Leo Zumbusch, the announced topic was "Pain and Its Effects on Neuro-Surgery,"[26] but the message to the students was "Langemarck." He urged them to refrain from thinking of their own suffering and pain caused by the current economic depression and social unrest, and remember instead "the fallen at Langemarck . . . who remained true until death for the Fatherland." The glory of Langemarck was thus set in opposition to the present unheroic spirit.

A plea for contemporary German youth to imitate their heroic predecessors was also made by Rector Paul Simon of the theological faculty at Tübingen in 1932. The occasion, ironically perhaps, was the celebration of the two-hundredth anniversary of George Washington's birthday and the conferral of an honorary degree on United States Ambassador Dr. Sackett. The rector expressed the hope that the recipient of the degree would proclaim back in America that "our academic youth, inspired by the same spirit (of high idealism), will always be prepared to offer themselves on the altar of the Fatherland."[27] Such glorification of the role of youth in achieving German national greatness was to be continued in the Third Reich by Adolf Hitler:

---

[24]Friedrich Meinecke, *The German Catastrophe* (Cambridge MA: Harvard University Press, 1950) 43.

[25]*Münchener Universitätsreden*, #15. (München: Max Huber Verlag, 1925). Hereinafter these speeches are referred to as *MU*.

[26]*MU* #26.

[27]*Tübinger Chronik*, 23 February 1932.

The youth is the stone which is to go to the building of our new Reich! You are greater Germany! On you is being formed the community of the German people. Before the single leader there stands a Reich; before the single Reich stands a people, and before the single people stands German youth! . . . In you will and shall be completed that for which generations and centuries have striven, Germany![28]

Is it not significant that the "values" of the German national tradition, which meant so much to the professors in the 1920s, were identical with those articulated by the leader of Nazism? Although I would not claim that they had in mind the same kind of implementation that Hitler had, it does seem legitimate to note their promotion of a "heroic" future regime, and their repeated comparisons of it to the weak and uninspiring Weimar government.

The period from 1925 to 1933 was crucial in the history of the Republic. Attempts were made to stabilize the government and to achieve a wholesome economy by including the various parties in the Cabinet; they met with mixed success. The professors, for their part, did nothing to assist in this task. On the contrary, they kept up a barrage against the Weimar Republic, constantly referred to it as weak, un-German, even criminal—altogether an *Unrechtsstaat*. They refused to be the bridge builders that Meinecke had hopefully envisioned, and by their negativity they helped the radical Right undo the coalition governments.

The professors were convinced that true German culture must not be derailed by new political forms out of harmony with its tradition. To them the unity of the German people was linked to the degree of conformity maintained by them with their cultural mission. Faithfulness to the "spirit" of the race and efforts to preserve it would, in their thinking, eventually redeem the nation. They would simply wait it out until the proper German state evolved—proper, that is, to the German *Kulturmission*.

They were right in their belief that the German people would not be satisfied with the Republic. They were right in thinking that German national consciousness would outlive the Weimar interlude. Where they were wrong was in their refusal to assume responsibility for offering a viable alternative to a weak and unstable society. Where they were wrong was in failing to anticipate that their aggressive nationalism was a key that would unlock the door to National Socialism in 1933.

---

[28]Norman H. Baynes, ed., *The Speeches of Adolf Hitler*, vol. 1 (New York: Oxford University Press, 1942) 551.

Chapter Two

The Power of Rhetoric

The rhetoric evidenced both in language and in symbolic actions by the Weimar professors belied their claims to be "above politics." Mention their names to any of their former colleagues and students and one hears the spontaneous response: "Ja, Deutschnational!" Only occasionally does one hear, "Ja, Demokratsch," and even less often—and in a different tone of voice—"Ja, Socialistisch!" How do we reconcile this easy identification of the political affiliation of the professors with their own assertion that they remained apolitical because involvement in political issues would prejudice their "unbiased scholarly achievement"? Were they, in fact, apolitical?

The attempt to reconstruct a particular intellectual climate is a difficult and dangerous historical task. The assumption that the intellectual climate explains the actions of persons is even more dangerous. Certainly, we do not usually decide on a specific political action because of a clear philosophical goal, but no one can contest the fact that beneath the choices made on the basis of economic betterment, political power, or social prestige lies a value system. The value system is imbedded in the tradition of a people, and the handing on of that tradition by educators is one of the basic reasons for having schools and universities. But handing on the tradition is not the full task; exploration and criticism of the tradition are the other side of the coin.

In the 1920s one finds a perception of the German tradition articulated by a group of journalists and publicists known, in retrospect, as the "Conservative Revolutionists." This was the name given to the circle around Arthur Moeller van den Bruck and, in its post-World War I phase, dates from the publication of his book, *Das Dritte Reich (The Third Reich)*, in 1923.[1] It was

---

[1]Arthur Moeller van den Bruck, *Germany's Third Empire*, trans. E. O. Lorimer (London: Allen and Unwin, 1934). The prewar use of the term *Conservative Revolution*

not an academic or university-based operation, but was the work of journalists and publicists, many of whom were looked upon with a certain disdain by the professors. Yet the resemblance between the two groups of conservatives is startling. In addition to Moeller van den Bruck, the group included Gerhard Gunther, Ernst and Georg Junger, August Winnig, Othmar Spann, Oswald Spengler, and Carl Schmitt.

Because their language, especially their metaphors, is so similar to that found in the professors' speeches of the time, it is useful to consider some of their writings. They shed light on the cultural context within which the academic leaders were speaking and make it possible to understand more fully the import of their words. The main elements of the rhetoric they share are: *Reich, Führer* (Leader), and *Kulturmission.*

The title of Moeller van den Bruck's major work gives us a clear statement of his political philosophy. The "Third Reich" was a concept of a medieval political theorist by the name of Joachim of Flora. In his understanding of the political order, linked (as was common by the medievalists) to the providential order that governed all things, the first "Reich" or "Kingdom" had been that of God the Father, the second that of Christ the Son, and the third would be that of the Holy Spirit. This basically religious projection is found in many historical works of the medieval period; man's journey is from the pre-Christian (Hebrew) age, through the Christian era, to the fullness of the Spirit in a third age. Underneath such a view of history lies a basic assumption of the unity of the human race, a common origin and destiny, and a common myth that binds the different ages together into a meaningful whole.

It was by analogy to this order that Moeller van den Bruck explained his political theory. The first kingdom or Reich was that of Charlemagne (Karl der Grosse to the Germans), the second that of Bismarck, and the third would be a mystical synthesis of all the Germanic values in a new political form.[2] There was no specific political action suggested by Moeller or by his associates for bringing about this new Reich; instead, the men of the Conservative Revolu-

---

refers to Paul Lagarde and Julius Langbehn. There are several good studies of this movement: Klemens von Klemperer, *Germany's New Conservatism* (Princeton: Princeton University Press, 1962); Fritz Stern, *The Politics of Cultural Despair* (Berkeley: University of California Press, 1961); James Michael Rhodes, "The Conservative Revolution in Germany: Myths of Contracted Reality" (Ph.D. dissertation, University of Notre Dame, 1969). Rhodes analyzes the use of the term *movement* for the Conservative Revolutionaries, maintaining that the writers found their unity in reaction against certain things, not in working together as a group.

[2]According to Rhodes, Moeller van den Bruck used the term *Third Reich* as a symbol of fulfillment that would be impossible to achieve ("The Conservative Revolution," 176-77).

tion—much like a demolition crew—did the work of preparing for the new builders. They spoke and wrote against the liberal and democratic institutions of Western parliamentary government as valueless and without cultural meaning. They fought "rationalism" because it assumed that man was basically good and governed by reason whereas they believed he was corrupt, irrational, and pusillanimous. Only suffering and self-conquest could redeem European society which, according to Moeller, had lost its conscience. "This lack of conscience dominates us; it dominates Europe; it dominates the world."[3]

The weekly journal of the movement was entitled *Gewissen* (Conscience), and it hammered away at the theme of European decadence. Weakness, corruption, compromise, petty venality—these are the sins of the "democratic," bourgeois West. The Conservatives called for a revival of strength, heroism, a sense of community, order in one's work and in all phases of civic life; these they called "German" virtues.

The extent to which such ideas were current among intellectuals in the postwar years is indicated by the fact that one of the early subscribers to *Gewissen* was the author Thomas Mann. He had seen the war as an answer to Europe's yearning for a moral cleansing—witness the theme of *The Magic Mountain*.[4] Mann's support was short-lived, however. In 1922 he rejected the Conservative Revolution and became a supporter of the Republic. *Gewissen* flourished from 1920 to 1927; at that time it was succeeded by *Die Tat*, but the movement had lost some of its general appeal because of improvements in the political and economic life of the Republic. However, it was revived after Stresemann's death in 1929 and some of its energies and ideas fed into the National Socialist movement.[5] Moeller himself had committed suicide in 1925, but between 1929 and 1933 his main works went through several reprintings. According to Fritz Stern, Moeller's idea of the Third Reich "constituted the most powerful myth of the antirepublican forces."[6]

Another facet of the ideology of the Conservative Revolution was the emphasis on the role of the hero who would be an intrinsic part of the Third Reich. He, *der Führer*, would come and lead the people into the promised land of renewed German greatness. This theme was developed, for example, in a speech

---

[3]*Gewissen*, 24 June 1919, as quoted in Stern, *Cultural Despair*, 228.

[4]Thomas Mann, *The Magic Mountain*, trans. H. T. Lowe-Porter (New York: Heritage Press, 1962).

[5]Stern, *Cultural Despair*, 206. See also Kurt Sontheimer, "Tatkreis," *Vierteljahrshefte für Zeitgeschichte* 7:3 (July 1959). *Der Ring* was another journal of the movement after 1928.

[6]Stern, *Cultural Despair*, 296.

by Oswald Spengler, author of the famous *Decline of the West,* to the students of the University of Munich in 1924.[7] Parliamentary democracy was totally unsuited to the German people, he said, because it lacked the necessary reliance on a hero that was demanded by the German character. He complained that the five years of the Weimar Republic had been "five years without action, decision, thought, or taking a stand on anything," and he attributed this to the basic trust in the equality of men and in their ability to govern themselves. He urged the students to resist the tide of decadent culture exemplified in the West—which was doomed to disappear—and to reassert a world view (*Weltanschauung*) based on Germany's heroic past. To do this they would need a leader who could unite the people, a man who would be "above party," and a form of State that would be worthy to carry forward such a heroic past into the future of the race.

The *Reich*, the Leader, the *Kulturmission*—when these concepts were combined in a myth that gave hope for a better future, there was no possibility of accepting a democratic parliamentary republic as the German State. It was "no true German State"; it was an *Unrechtsstaat*. The appearance of these same ideas—*Reich*, Leader, *Kulturmission*—in the speeches the university rectors gave at the annual celebrations of the Foundation of the Reich is striking.

I

Although the adoption date of the Weimar constitution—11 August 1919—had been designated as a national holiday, as late as 1925 the American consul general in Munich commented, "The call for the celebration of the sixth anniversary of the adoption of the Weimar constitution went almost unheeded in Munich and its immediate neighborhood."[8] On the other hand, just the year before, the Academic Senate at the University of Munich had voted to reestablish the celebration of the Foundation of the Reich, 19 January 1871.[9]

---

[7]Oswald Spengler, "Politische Pflichten der deutschen Jugend," *Politische Schriften* (München, 1933) as quoted in Kurt Sontheimer, *Antidemokratisches Denken in der Weimarer Republik* (München: Nymphenburger Verlag, 1962) 188. See also Spengler, *Neubau des Deutschen Reiches* (München: Beck, 1924).

[8]G. B. Curtis to Department of State, Washington D.C., 14 August 1925 (State Department Microcopy #336. File #862.41-862.4646).

[9]A description of these celebrations at the University of Heidelberg is given in the study done by Arye Zvi Carmon, "The University of Heidelberg and National Socialism" (Ph.D. dissertation, University of Wisconsin, 1974). He points out that there were four large celebrations each year and all had to do with the Reich. As at other universities, these elaborate rituals were in stark contrast to the absence of celebration of the Weimar Republic.

On the first anniversary after the celebration had been restored—19 January 1925—the rector, Professor Eduard Schwartz, took great pains to explain the seriousness of the Senate's decision to reintroduce the national holiday of the Reich.[10] He said that they had done so in order to honor all those who had given their lives for the Kaiser and the Reich, not only in war but also in the reconstruction of the State and in the liberation of it from "unGerman criminals." He spoke in condemnation of the present leaders who opposed the development of the *Freikorps* (Free Corps)—a paramilitary group that was growing despite the prohibition of such groups by the Versailles treaty and the efforts of the Weimar government to comply with the terms. Schwartz thus "celebrated" those who were defying the treaty and the Republic.

The renewed celebration of the foundation of the *Reich* was, in itself, an affront to the Republic. When coupled with the absence of any celebration on 11 August, the national constitutional holiday, the impact was even greater.

The professors clearly were as much concerned with building up the myth of the Reich as they were in undermining the Republic. They were not only antidemocratic; they were pro-something. They were not exactly against freedom; they were for unity. They believed in "scholarship"; they specialized in *Wissenschaft*. This should have forced upon them a greater precision in the use of terms like *Reich, Führer,* and *Kulturmission,* but in fact only contributed further to the distortions. Their dedication to such myths had more than a touch of the irrational. The day would come when their rhetoric would be used in the service of National Socialism. That is why it is important to examine their language closely and critically.

In the use of this noun *Reich* there are ambiguities. Sometimes it is a pseudoreligious reference to that inner kingdom in which the German people find their unity. It is a concretization of the Kingdom of God; in it the Germans are all one. This use is found in both medieval Catholic and early Lutheran tradition. At other times the term *Reich* points to the actual kingdom of Charles the Great, of the Holy Roman Emperor, or of Bismarck. The distinction between these two meanings of the term is not always clearly indicated, and that may be intentional. Speeches given by the university professors on patriotic occasions are not expected to be analytical but rather inspirational. The political instability of Germany in the early 1920s cried out for an ideology that would restore a sense of unity and purpose. The pain of the nation must be given a meaning, and that meaning would be partly spiritual and partly political.

---

[10]Eduard Schwartz, "Rede zur Reichsgrundungsfeier der Universität München," *MU #2.* See also the protocols for the Senate meetings, University of Munich, 1924-1926, Archives of the University of Munich.

At times the thrust was clearly religious. Karl Adam, a Catholic theologian at Tübingen, may shock us with his reflections on the special "mission" of the Germans with reference to the Kingdom of God. In his work, *Christ and the Modern Mind* (1928), he insisted that the "West" (including Germany, as distinguished from the "West" of Spengler) had a special mission in the divine plan and that it was the "specially chosen" of Christ. Stephen, the first Christian martyr, was a Greek and not a Jew, a Westerner according to Adam. It was the youthful Germanic tribes that broke into the decadent Roman Empire, bringing their "youthful power and disposition of heroism" to the spirit of Jesus. The triumph of this combination is seen in the person of the emperor: "It was not long before the cross shone forth in the crown of the Roman Emperor of the German Nation."[11]

The Protestant theologian Wilhelm Stapel saw in the search for a new Reich a desire on the part of twentieth-century man to end the dualism between the sacred and the secular.[12] Having lost the medieval model, based as it was on the unity of the Christian faith, man was wandering among the pluralistic forces of modern times and could find no resolution to his need for integration.

Other authors make similar points. "The old mold of the Reich as the *sacrum imperium* had become anachronistic in a world of secularism," but the search to find a substitute was both political and religious.[13] Franz Schauwecker actually used the terms *Kingdom of God* and *Kingdom of the German people* synonymously.[14] One of the professors at Greifswald University, Otto Procksch, expressed the link between the notion of *Reich* and the desire for a leader in explicitly religious terms: "If the German way and the Christian faith will be joined together then we shall be saved, then will we work with our hands and await the day when the German hero will come. He will come as prophet or as king."[15]

----

[11]Karl Adam, *Christ and the Western Mind* (New York: Macmillan Company, 1930) 10, 12. Adam does protect the Christian notion of a transcendent God and refuses to place the ultimate value in blood. He specifically rejects the racism of Chamberlain, yet holds on to a unique role for Germans in the redemptive work of Christ. Out of context, he could be seen as a nationalistic supporter of the unique mission of German Christians.

[12]Sontheimer, *Antidemokratisches Denken*, 283.

[13]William J. Bossenbrook, *The German Mind* (Detroit: Wayne State University Press, 1961) 325.

[14]Sontheimer, *Antidemokratisches Denken*, 285.

[15]Helmut Kuhn, *Die deutsche Universität im Dritten Reich* (München: R. Piper and Co., 1966) 27.

The confusion of religious and political language is more than accidental, and it is highly dangerous if accepted uncritically. In an attempt to solidify the cultural or spiritual bonds of the "nation," many speakers and authors failed to clarify the relationship that existed between such bonds and the structures of political life. Friedrich Meinecke wrote, "By cleansing the idea of the nation of everything political and infusing it instead with all the spiritual achievements that have been won, the national idea was raised to the sphere of religion and the eternal."[16]

An understanding, then, of this concept of the nation as a cultural and religious reality, above and beyond the reach of politics, is a prerequisite to dealing with the historical manifestation of the nation, that is, the Reich. In the university speeches of the 1925-1933 period, there are still occasional references to the Medieval Empire as the climactic realization of Germanic culture, but most of the speakers deal more directly with the Reich of Bismarck. Concretely, they are talking about Germany, the nation-state, with its geographic boundaries of 1871-1918. The sphere of religion and the eternal suddenly seems politically visible.

In an address delivered at the University of Munich on 19 January 1925, Professor Eduard Schwartz was explicit about his demands for the restoration of Germany's prewar boundaries, which he considered those of the true Reich. He spoke disparagingly of the new nations created out of former Habsburg lands—the lands of the Reich. They are "incapable of self-government and incapable of learning anything." A certain nostalgia colors his references to his days of teaching in Strasbourg before the war, when it was under German control and he could teach "German knowledge" in "German freedom." He called for student response to the German nation's need to reassert the true spirit of Bismarck's time. He concluded with the hope that the day would soon dawn when such a spirit would be theirs and "the classrooms and laboratories will again be united with the drill field and the training ship."[17]

In June of the same year, the university had a special celebration in honor of the One Thousand Year Anniversary of the Rhineland. Again, attention was focused on a part of the Reich that had been lost as a result of the Versailles treaty. According to Hermann Oncken, the speaker of the occasion, it must be

---

[16]Quoted by Fritz Stern, "The Political Consequences of the Unpolitical German," *History, a Meridian Periodical* 3 (1960): 129.

[17]*MU #2*. One can appreciate Schwartz's references to Strasbourg after reading John Craig's *Scholarship and Nation Building: The Universities of Strasbourg and Alsatian Society, 1870-1939* (Chicago: University of Chicago Press, 1984). Both the Germans and the French saw the university there at different times as an instrument for the promotion of their national goals.

reunited to Germany.[18] Oncken's unenthusiastic attitude toward the Weimar Republic becomes more understandable when one looks at his deep attachment to the historic Reich.

In 1925 the Rhineland was still under Allied occupation. According to the provisions of Versailles, it was to be evacuated gradually: the first zone around Cologne was to be occupied for five years (until 1 December 1925), the second at Coblentz for ten years (actually evacuated 30 November 1929), and the third at Mainz for fifteen years (actually evacuated 30 June 1930). This arrangement and the demilitarization of the Rhine had been concessions on the part of France, whose first demand had been for annexation of the left bank of the Rhine. Now, in 1925, there were Separatist movements in the area, and the Germans were accusing the French of supporting them.

Against this background Oncken presented the students with a history of the Rhineland that allowed for no French claims to the area whatsoever. Beginning with Charles the Great (a German, from his point of view) the Rhine had been a German river. Always, "the entire German fate had been decided, so it appeared, in the fate of the Rhineland." He spoke with pride and joy of the entry of the German army into France in August 1870 and contrasted it with Germany's unhappy position at this moment in history. From 1871 to 1914, he claimed, the French had sought every possible chance to take the Rhineland and, not succeeding at Versailles in their attempts to secure outright annexation, they were trying to do it by "indirect penetration." The French, Oncken insisted, had nothing to fear from Germany; on the contrary, if the nations of the world were concerned about promoting peace, they should protect the Rhine and Germany against France.

Oncken's ostensibly historical treatment of the question must be read in conjunction with the introductory remarks made by the rector, Dr. Leopold Wenger,[19] in order to assess the full impact of his words on the students. The responsibility for reuniting the Rhineland to the other German States and thus reconstituting the full Reich of Bismarck is left to the students; an older generation is passing on the torch of German nationalism. The rector left no one in doubt that he was speaking of more than a mystical sense of brotherhood when he spoke of their "brothers from the Rhine" as sufferers and even martyrs. He was proposing a reunion of all who spoke the German tongue and projecting a truly "cultural" basis for a nation.

---

[18]Hermann Oncken, "Jahrtausendfeier des Rheinlandes," *MU* #4 (1925).

[19]Ibid., intro.

Professor Oncken was again chosen as orator for the celebration of the Foundation of the Reich in January 1926.[20] He urged his audience to examine their own personal understanding of the Reich and what it symbolized. He called their attention to the "moral power" inherent in that form of the German state.

> In the historic moment in which the German nation stands today, we have let our glances wander on the Memorial Day of the Foundation of the Reich to the tasks, the possibilities, the hopes of the future. Let us once more look, from the depths of today's "unfreedom" back toward the Reich which we once occupied, and then we shall be overwhelmingly conscious of how wide and steep is the way that lies before us. . . . As for our goal and for the winning back of German freedom, fitting are the words which Bismarck spoke in the year 1868: "If we achieve our goal in the next generation, that will be a great thing; if we can reach it sooner that will be an unhoped-for gift of grace from God."

The achievement of the Bismarckian Reich had been, for Oncken, a gift of grace from God—and one that he undoubtedly hoped to see repeated.

At the University of Heidelberg there was a similar call to cooperate with that sense of mission and to work toward the reconstruction of the Reich, "the pride of our past and the treasure we hoard in the present."[21] In January 1929 Professor von Schubert thus urged the students at the Foundation of the Reich celebration to undertake the work of winning back the 1871 boundaries.

> Help to keep a faithful watch at our borders, at our Rhine; our university has become a border university and has received a legacy from Strasbourg; let us always look over to the Pfalz and the Saar with the thought of an obligation and let us not forget the heavier than ever, the endangered, the struggling Ostmark in which the work of Frederick the Great lies in ruin. And then a great number of you will take up an official career and step into the direct service of the State. The word service is not popular today—not considered important! You will love it if you permeate it with obedience, from which it is inseparable, with the basic German virtue, with loyalty which supported the whole essence of feudalism. . . . Let us, both young and old generation, honor the teachings of our great history. Let us build the bridge from the old to the new Reich.

The image of building a bridge from the old Reich to a new Reich is a common one. Was this not to be the "Third Reich"?

Perhaps the most convincing proof that indeed the image of the Third Reich was being concretized for their generation can be found in the work of Professor Johannes Haller of Tübingen. His major publication, *The Epochs of German His-*

---

[20]Hermann Oncken, "Deutsche Vergangenheit und deutsche Zukunft," *MU* #6 (1926).

[21]Hans v. Schubert, "Altes und Neues Reich deutscher Nation," *Heidelberg Universitätsreden* #6 (18 January 1929); hereinafter referred to as *HU*.

tory,[22] tells the tale. There are three editions of this work: 1923, 1939, and 1950. In the first edition Haller decried the defeat of Germany in World War I and the "present events" (1923) that were resulting in its devastation; he ended the foreword with an expression of hope that Germany would one day rise again to her rightful place among the nations of the world. This edition went only as far as the triumph of Bismarck, seeing in it a peak of German history.

In 1939, as Hitler was embarking on his conquest of the European continent, Haller wrote a preface to the new edition of his work in which he rejoiced that "The Day" of German restoration had come much sooner than he had dared to hope. The text was now extended beyond Bismarck to the present time (1939) and the chapter headings were entitled in a way that reveals Haller's point of view:

> Years of Powerlessness, Need and Disgrace
> (Weimar)
> Victory of National Thoughts (1933)
> The Liberation—National Socialist Regime
> (Since 1933)

There was in 1939, according to Haller, a new epoch in German history—the Third Reich of Hitler.

Although Haller died in 1947, he had prepared a revision of his work that appeared in 1950. This edition has the same foreword as the 1923 edition and the chapters added in the 1939 edition have been deleted. Haller had witnessed the bridge built from the old Reich to the new one, but he had also seen it destroyed. His historical consciousness was so dependent on the concept of the German Reich as the embodiment of the German nation that his history had to be rewritten as the Reich appeared and disappeared.

In another work he was explicit about his motive in writing history:

> One will find it only natural that it is above all the thought of a vital future for Germany which has led me to take up my pen—the thought of the youth of Germany who, we hope, will find once again what their fathers have lost. May these pages contribute to a deepening of the insight that in the life of a people and a State no task can be solved (and so also not the question of life for Germany and its position *vis-à-vis* France) without a clear recognition from the pages of history of its origin and growth.[23]

What, we may ask, had their fathers lost? Was it not the great German Reich?

------

[22]Johannes Haller, *Epochen der deutschen Geschichte* (Stuttgart: J. G. Cotta, 1923 and 1939; Stuttgart: Port Verlag, 1950).

[23]Johannes Haller, *Tausend Jahre deutsche-franzosischer Beziehungen* (Stuttgart: J. G. Cotta, 1930).

Can one place much trust in this depiction of a thousand years of German-French relations when the author says that he is writing it precisely to inspire young Germans to revise the boundaries set by the Versailles treaty?

The Reich, then, was a vision that captivated professors as well as publicists. Although one cannot claim that all who used the term meant the same thing, nonetheless such ambiguity only intensified the problem. It has been said that the ambiguity of language is one of the major problems in analyzing the objectives of the Conservative Revolutionaries.[24] Did similar ambiguity on the part of the professors not have an impact on their listeners or readers? Having grown accustomed to the rhetoric of their professors, which promoted a new and glorious Reich, was it not more likely that the students would accept the goals proclaimed in the language of Hitler?

One may certainly ask whether the absence of such precision of thought can be tolerated in an academic community as easily as in journalistic circles. If the Reich was intended to be understood as the eschatological "age of the Spirit"—an unattainable but real manifestation of God toward which the people would struggle—then the speakers needed to set the theological groundwork for their announced goal. They ought not to have illustrated the concept by reference to the Rhineland, the German lands in the east, or the Reich of Bismarck. Such concrete examples used to summon enthusiasm for the Reich belie a purely religious or spiritual symbol. Here acceptance of a myth carries with it significant moral responsibility.

II

In many instances this dedication to the realization of the Reich was linked to strong praise for the founder of the Second Reich, Otto von Bismarck. Just as it is hard to separate the German people's calls for a "spiritual unity" from a political movement toward an actual Reich, so it is practically impossible to know how close an identification was made in most people's minds between the Leader (*der Führer*) and Bismarck.

There was in the universities of the Weimar period a veritable cult of Bismarck; his statesmanship was continually contrasted with the weak, indecisive leadership of the Republic. A strong leader was necessary to the notion of the Reich because it was in him that the spiritual unity of the people would be integrated and articulated. He would not let things drift, nor allow the ups and downs of political parties to determine values. The creativity of the nation had

---

[24]Rhodes, "The Conservative Revolution," addresses the problem of ambiguity in the language of the Conservative Revolutionaries. See also von Klemperer, *Germany's New Conservatism*, 123-24.

been exemplified in this heroic figure—Bismarck—and the youth of the nation should now seek a new leader who would carry on the task.

Significant attention was paid to Bismarck in the courses offered in the universities, the lectures given to outsiders, the articles published by the faculties, and the speeches given on important occasions. There was no other historical personage—Frederick the Great, Napoleon, Julius Caesar—who got equal time with the Iron Chancellor. And there is an aura of hagiography around all that was written and said of him.

The cult of Bismarck was deeply rooted in the historical thought of the Weimar period. As a discipline that prides itself on objectivity, history obviously failed at this crucial moment. A detailed study of the professors on the history faculty of the University of Munich (Konrad Beyerle, Max Buchner, Michael Doberl, Erich Marcks, Karl Alexander von Müller, and Hermann Oncken) has demonstrated that, with the exception of Beyerle, they all reinforced the myths I have been discussing: *Reich*, Leader, *Kulturmission*.[25]

Even Beyerle saw the Republic as an "unfortunate consequence" of the war and the revolution of 1918; he differed from his colleagues only in his view that it had to be accepted since history is irreversible. Beyerle was the only one who dared to criticize Bismarck.[26] The others saw him as the kind of leader desperately needed by Germany at this time. Oncken, according to Weisz, constantly posed the question when trying to make a judgment: "What would Bismarck offer as the solution?" Even when he finally accepted the Weimar Republic as the only viable alternative, he clothed his decision in the legitimating remark that "Bismarck would have done the same thing."[27]

These historians saw the Reich as the ideal form of the German State and hoped that some day the monarchy would be restored. They presented the Weimar Republic as the antithesis of the high point of recent German history—that is, the Reich of Bismarck. Consequently, their interpretations of the war, the treaty, and the creators of the Republic were all colored by a basic conviction that true German greatness could never be achieved in a parliamentary democracy with a party system that failed to reflect the unity of the German nation.

As a result, homage to the authoritarian chancellor was extreme. Karl Alexander von Müller, in his biography of Bismarck, suggests him as a model for men of the 1920s who aspired to leadership: "His picture hangs before us when we

---

[25]Christoph Weisz, *Geschichtsauffassung und politisches Denken Münchener Historiker der Weimarer Zeit* (Berlin: Duncker and Humblot, 1970) 210-67.

[26]Ibid., 126. See the whole section on Bismarck, 125-30.

[27]Ibid., 127.

hope that the political creativity of our people has not been lost, and that a day will come again when it will be concentrated in a great leader."[28] Marcks goes even further. Bismarck was "the genius of all geniuses" and "the highest of all our heroes."[29] He identifies him with the great Reich itself and the very essence of Germanness. "He had become Prussia and he would become the *Reich*." Finally, Buchner, who as a Catholic might be expected to be less well disposed toward the author of the Kulturkampf, considered that anyone who criticized the leadership of Bismarck was a "traitor" to the Fatherland.[30]

The link between this idealization of Bismarck and the anti-Republicanism of the professors is not hard to establish. Bismarck had made it his policy to avoid true parliamentarianism. He typified the kind of leader who did not consider himself accountable to the people nor to their elected delegates. For such an authoritarian leader to be made the model for Germany in the Weimar period betrayed a basic mistrust of democracy and a strong desire to be led rather than to lead. If Germany were to discover a new Bismarck to lead them out of the present weakness, then there would be clear support for this man from the professorial ranks.

As far back as 1917 Max Weber, writing in the *Frankfürter Zeitung*, had called attention to the unfortunate effects of Bismarck's authoritarianism.

> Bismarck left behind him as his political heritage a nation without any political education, far below the level which, in this respect, it had reached twenty years earlier. Above all, he left behind a nation without any political will, accustomed to having the great statesman at its head look after its policy for it. Moreover . . . he left "a nation accustomed to submit, under the label of constitutional monarchy, to anything which was decided for it."[31]

Friedrich Meinecke had also been alert to this critical weakness in the Reich and deplored Bismarck's long-range influence: "The nation's own achievement . . . was too small. It was too much the instrument in the hands of a mighty leader. It still had to become . . . energetic and mature by virtue of its own activity."[32]

Although this evaluation had been written in 1914, the leaders of the academic community in 1928 were still rejoicing in the kind of leadership that Bis-

---

[28]Ibid.

[29]Ibid., 128.

[30]Ibid., 126.

[31]As quoted in J. P. Mayer, *Max Weber and German Politics* (London: Faber and Faber, 1944) 59.

[32]Friedrich Meinecke, *Der deutsche Erhebung von 1914*, as quoted in Richard Sterling, *Ethics in a World of Power* (Princeton: Princeton University Press, 1958) 127.

marck had exemplified. The insights of the eminent sociologist of Munich and the equally well-known historian in Berlin were ignored by the Bismarck worshipers among the historians. Instead, the professors continued to use the image of the Iron Chancellor as a norm against which to measure the weak, struggling, and inefficient men of Weimar. In doing so they inspired their audiences to seek the new Führer who would save them by creating a new Reich.

III

Finally, the Republic was unsatisfactory because it was incapable of being the embodiment of the German *Kulturmission*. Nowhere is the difficulty of translation more obvious than in the attempt to render the German words *Kultur*, *Kulturmission*, and *Kulturstaat* into English. Fritz Stern has addressed this problem and has some helpful comments:

> For a century or more the German term *"Kultur"* had a reverential connotation that the simple English word "culture" cannot render. It was invested with the awe and reverence that Germans felt, or thought they should feel, for the diverse creations of the spirit, for the mystery of the arts that to so many possessed a voice as tender and as powerful as religion itself. This idealization of culture inspired and guided the great intellectual and scientific achievements of modern Germany.[33]

This Germanic preoccupation with the notion of culture, cultural values, and the means of communicating these values—which are, by definition, deeply imbedded in the people (*Volk*)—goes far back into the history of the nation. Herder had articulated it well in the eighteenth century and had explained it in universal terms. He believed that *each* nation (not in the sense of nation-state, but of the people bound together in cultural union) had its unique cultural forms "that rise spontaneously out of the spiritual consciousness of a people."[34]

This notion had been further elaborated by the Romantics of the early nineteenth century who defined culture as the expression of the "creative force of the *Volkgeist* (spirit of the people)." Culture thus became, in the German understanding of it, the cumulative product of the creative moments in a people's history, spiritual in nature but needing institutionalization if it were to be of permanent value to mankind.[35]

It is at this point that the spiritual and political spheres intersect. To institutionalize the cultural values of a people, the State comes into existence. At

---

[33]Stern, "The Political Consequences," 106.

[34]Bossenbrook, *The German Mind*, 349.

[35]Ibid.

the very moment in German history when the forces of nationalism were moving toward a new mode of expression, the political complexities of post-Napoleonic Europe led gradually toward the formation of the German nation-state. Later, under the leadership of Bismarck, it took the form of the Second Reich. The State was understood as the political structure destined to support and preserve the cultural values of the nation.

It was Johann Gottlieb Fichte, one of the first philosophy professors at the University of Berlin, who coined the word *Kulturstaat* to describe the nature of the State.[36] He did it long before the realization of the Reich under Bismarck, but he furnished the concept in terms that the Germans would later use to understand their experience of becoming a modern nation-state. His colleague, Wilhelm von Humboldt, the founder of the University of Berlin, was eloquent in his defense of cultural freedom against the censorship of a paternalistic and authoritarian government, for he insisted on the priority of the people's cultural values over the security of the government or the State.

Ringer has suggested that through a certain unwritten agreement these men in the early nineteenth century secured the collaboration of the State in their educational mission by making it clear to the State that it could find its own legitimacy only in being a trustworthy vehicle for the culture (spiritual values) of the nation (people). Germany, in the time of Fichte and von Humboldt, was not yet a nation-state; hence the nation had to define itself in cultural terms, for they were the source of its unity. As a result of this historical fact, the "nation, and through it, the State, were defined as creatures and as agents of the mandarins' cultural ideals."[37] That is what it meant to be a *Kulturstaat*.

The Germans found a uniqueness in their possession of a *Kulturstaat* and preferred it to a State founded on a "contract theory," or a "general will," or any other political concept. Nevertheless, as time went on and technological and industrial changes altered the character of political and social life, the "cultural values" of the "nation" became more difficult to define. Immigration and emigration, mixed marriages, and increased economic and social relationships of an international dimension all made it increasingly unclear as to who constituted the "nation" and whose "cultural values" were to be embodied in the State. It is precisely in the Germans' inability to confront this chang-

---

[36]Fritz K. Ringer, *The Decline of the German Mandarins* (Cambridge MA: Harvard University Press, 1969) 115.

[37]Ibid., 116.

ing scene that one finds the cause of their political failure in the Weimar period.[38] The professors shared in this failure.

As late as 1933 the universities were still oriented toward the "cultural mission." At the annual foundation of the Reich celebration in Munich, Professor Heinrich Günter belabored the point so often made before: the youth must seek out the ephemeral "German spirit" that had inspired the Reich and find a new form in which to embody it. He asserted his confidence that they would find the necessary inspiration in the words "*Deutschland über Alles*," which, he felt, contain a "well-ordered pride in the German's cultural mission."[39]

If one accepts the notion that the State's primary function is to serve as "an instrumentality to realize cultural objectives," it becomes, according to Friedrich Meinecke, the chosen means for "realizing and preserving the spiritual and intellectual endowments of man" and, as such, must have power and authority. Further, such a goal requires institutions, and these must be "pervaded by the life-stream of the national community and its social groups." Thus the people (*Volk*) and the society (*Gemeinschaft*) determine the nature of these institutions and the character of the State. "This stream of life," Meinecke continues, "produces the spiritual and moral energies and goals which support the power of the State and exalt the State itself into an idea, into one of the greatest spiritual powers of cultural life."[40]

What may appear here as undue exaltation of the State at the expense of the individual is counteracted in Meinecke's thought (and in the whole Kantian-Fichtean tradition) by the moral restraints presumed to be operative in the exercise of power. While it is an anti-Rousseauean concept of the State, it is not necessarily a profascist one. The moral purpose that Meinecke attributed to

---

[38]Fritz Stern has expressed it well: "But the ideal of culture, once embodied in institutions, became more and more a passive appreciation of past creativity, and in time it degenerated into little more than the ritualistic repetition of phrases and pieties. Far more important than the decline was the impact that this veneration of culture had on German society, on politics, religion, and on what may be called the national self-image. . . . It fostered several political prejudices and positions, none favorable to the development of a democratic society or even to the growth of a cohesive nation. . . . There is pathos in the fact that the Germans used their greatest achievement, their culture, to augment and excuse their greatest failure, their politics" ("The Political Consequences," 106-107).

[39]Heinrich Gunter, "Das mittelalterliche Kaisertum," *MU* #27 (1933).

[40]On the thought of Meinecke, see Sterling, *Ethics;* Douglas Tobler, "German Historians and the Weimar Republic" (Ph.D. dissertation, University of Kansas, 1967); Philip Wolfson, "Friedrich Meinecke, 1882-1954," *Journal of the History of Ideas* 17:4 (October 1956): 511-25; and Robert Pois, "Friedrich Meinecke and German Politics in the Twentieth Century" (Ph.D. dissertation, University of Wisconsin, 1965).

the individual had its counterpart in the moral purpose of the State. When he later reflected on what he called *The German Catastrophe*, Meinecke still affirmed his faith in the separate path that Germany had followed (separate, that is, from the one taken in the Western nations after the French Revolution) and he blamed the "demonic forces of political power" on the "mass emotions and mass democracy which supported an irrational nationalism," and not on a notion of the State that gave it unlimited power to carry out the "mission" of its people.[41]

Meinecke is cited in this connection because, unlike the extreme German Nationalists in the universities, he was a supporter of the Republic—albeit only a "Republican of the Head." He was also a respected historian and political scientist, and his corpus of writings on the nature of the State is extensive. He struggled to articulate the special nature of German politics and the peculiar mission of its people, and his political theory deserves far more discussion than I can give it here. However, it seems clear that George Iggers is right when he claims: "Even after the catastrophes of Nazism and world war, Meinecke remained convinced that on the whole the nationalism of the German classical liberals, with their emphasis upon national power and the subordination of individual welfare to the higher needs of the nation, was right."[42] If this was true of a "Republican of the Head," how much better does it describe the thinking of the stubbornly anti-Weimar professors? Their identification of themselves as special "bearers of the culture" of the great German people gave them a particular function in the *Kulturstaat* that was above political parties and, to their satisfaction, "unpolitical." A State with so noble a mission deserved a fitting Reich in which to be embodied; it was impossible for a democratic State, so easily the prey of politicians, to carry on such a mission. Hence Weimar was an *Unrechtsstaat* (no true German state) and the German culture-mission needed a new home.

The concepts of a *Kultur* and *Kulturstaat* contain a fundamental assumption about the unity of the people. The *Volk* do not come into existence because they all live in one place or under one government—as one might think of the American people—but rather they were one before the State or even the nation was formed. *Einheit* (unity) is therefore a spiritual reality that is independent of law, geography, treaty, or citizenship. The German people are held together by deep cultural bonds and are, by nature, one.

---

[41]Friedrich Meinecke, *The German Catastrophe* (Cambridge MA: Harvard University Press, 1950) passim.

[42]George G. Iggers, *The German Conception of History* (Wesleyan CT: Wesleyan University Press, 1968) 225.

The reinforcement of this notion by the currents of romanticism in the nineteenth century had an added note: "by nature" came to mean for some writers a question of blood or race. This, of course, was not a line of thought restricted to Germans; the words of Comte Joseph de Gobineau and Houston Stewart Chamberlain were as powerfully racial as those of Julius Langbehn, Paul Lagarde, and Alfred Rosenberg.[43] What was decisive was the link that was forged between such an understanding of race and the fundamental definition of culture. When it turned out, as it did in Weimar, that many of the cultural innovators were of non-German background—often Jewish—it was only a brief step into the racist myth.

Reviewers of novels, plays, concerts, or art exhibits in the 1920s frequently used terms such as *bourgeois, decadent, Western, bolshevist, un-German*. Among the Conservatives who were seeking a restoration of German cultural greatness there was a repugnance for Weimar culture. That they often lumped *Western* and *bolshevist* together in their reviews suggests not so much a clear critical norm as a simple hatred for anything that did not embrace the values they identified with classical German learning and the basic instincts of the *Volk*. It was also common to see Weimar culture as Jewish.

A comment by Carl von Ossietzky in the left-wing periodical *Weltbühne* is humorous but probably on target:

> Cultural Bolshevism is when Conductor Klemperer takes tempi different from his colleague Furtwangler, when a painter sweeps color into his sunset not seen in Lower Pomerania, when one favors birth control, when one builds a house with a flat roof, when one shows a Caesarian birth on the screen, when one admires a performance of Charlie Chaplin and the mathematical wizardry of Albert Einstein, when one follows the democracy of the brothers Mann and when one enjoys the music of Hindemith and Kurt Weill—all that is cultural Bolshevism.[44]

---

[43]Paul Lagarde (1827-1891) was an Orientalist who occupied a chair at Göttingen and urged the elimination of all Semitic and Roman elements in German culture. See Koppel S. Pinson, *Modern Germany* (New York: The Macmillan Company, 1966) 271. Julius Langbehn (1851-1907) is best known for his *Rembrandt als Erzieher* (1890). According to Karl Dietrich Bracher, they found a devoted following among the German middle class (*The German Dictatorship* [New York: Praeger, 1970] 16). The best overall treatment of Langbehn and Lagarde is Stern, *Cultural Despair*. Alfred Rosenberg published his *Myth of the Twentieth Century* in 1930 and became Hitler's chief guide on racial policies. Count Joseph de Gobineau had written his *Essay on the Inequality of the Races of Man* (1853-1899) and Houston Stewart Chamberlain wrote *Foundations of the Nineteenth Century* (1899), which glorified the "creative culture" of the Aryan race. Thus the French and British made their contributions to what came to be considered a "German" phenomenon.

[44]Quoted in Istvan Deak, *Weimar Germany's Left-Wing Intellectuals* (Berkeley: University of California Press, 1968) 2.

True German culture would not admit this kind of discontinuity with the tradition. New cultural elements in German society were denied legitimacy. The unity of the nation required renewed emphasis on those historical moments when the cultural greatness of the German *Volk* had been uncontested.

The university community recognized this need by reinstituting the celebration of the Foundation of the Reich each year on January 19th. They made no effort to celebrate the national holiday commemorating the establishment of the Weimar Republic. Ritual actions are another form of language, and the professors' performance of them was consistent with the speeches given on such occasions.

Another sign of the intransigent devotion to the Reich and to Bismarck was the universities' attitude toward that most evocative of national symbols—the flag. To a person who has had the experience of living under only one flag, it is almost incomprehensible how deep the German feeling was in 1919 when it came time to choose a flag for the new government. In the National Assembly the Democrats urged the adoption of the black-red-gold colors that had marked the Frankfort Assembly and the liberal movements of the early nineteenth century. They saw this as a flag that would signify the "democracy" of the new Republic. Their opponents wanted the black-red-white of the old Reich, colors selected by Bismarck and proposed by him to Wilhelm I as a combination of the Prussian black and white and the Hanseatic or mercantile flag of red and white. Thus the Imperial flag was a symbol of the union of Prussia and Brandenburg, the core of the Second Reich.

The debate in 1919 was long and heated. Rejection of the black-red-white was, to the Conservatives, a rejection of tradition, a betrayal of those Germans who were now cut off from the rest by the territorial changes mandated at Versailles but who were still united in heart to the Reich. Further, it was a sign of the loss of the German people's sense of identity. It was, of course, exactly such a break with the imperial past that the Democrats were trying to symbolize by the adoption of a new flag. In the end the assembly voted for black-red-gold, but admitted the black-red-white as an "official" mercantile flag.[45]

Many of the German people, and many of the universities, simply refused to fly the flag of the Republic. They clung to the flags of their various *Lände* rather than acknowledge the Weimar Republic. Kahl, in his speech at the professors' 1926 meeting in Weimar, referred to the universities' attitude toward the flag: "[They did not have] . . . the heart and the mind for black-red-gold."[46]

---

[45]Hajo Holborn, *A History of Modern Germany, 1840-1945* (New York: Alfred A. Knopf, 1969) 202.

[46]Wilhelm Kahl, Friedrich Meinecke, and Gustav Radbruch, *Die deutschen Universitäten und der heutige Staat* (Tübingen: C. B. Mohr, 1926) 13.

In May of that same year the flag controversy broke out anew in government circles. An order went out to embassies and consulates abroad to fly the mercantile flag—the black-red-white—as well as the Republic's black-red-gold. The directive, understood to be expressive of the wish of President von Hindenburg, was sent out in the name of Dr. Luther, the chancellor. The sharpness with which the government was attacked in the Reichstag for having sent out this instruction revealed how near to the surface feelings were on this symbolic issue. Dr. Luther was voted out of office on May 12th, still not comprehending why the matter had become so explosive. Luther is supposed to have remarked to a party leader: "I do not understand how they could put a government out of office on account of such a bagatelle." To this statement he received the apt retort: "That's exactly why."[47]

If Luther did not grasp the popular feeling about the nation's symbol, there were others who did. Karl Vossler, a philologist of international reputation, was rector of the University of Munich that same year. Sensitive to the general currents of German Nationalism among the professors, he had hesitated about accepting the post. In a letter to the previous rector on 26 April 1926, Vossler had explained that his colleague Hermann Oncken had told him that he was being considered for the office of rector for the following year. He wanted to point out to those responsible for the appointment that he would be a bad choice since 1926-1927 was to be the Jubilee year of the university and his "politics" were not representative of the faculties, students, and officials of the university or of the ministry. He feared that the joy of the Jubilee year might be diminished by conflict.[48] After his election as rector, he took the question of flying the national flag to the Academic Senate.[49] Although the Republic had been proclaimed in 1919, the University of Munich had not yet raised its emblem on campus. Vossler now suggested that the Jubilee would be a suitable occasion for hoisting the black-red-gold. After extended debate, the professors agreed, but only on condition that it be flown together with the black-red-white (now the mercantile flag, but formerly that of the Reich) and the flags of Bavaria, Munich, and Landshut (the first location of the university). Perhaps the tenor of the debate on this matter can be gauged from the fact that one of his

---

[47]Erich Eyck, *A History of the Weimar Republic*, vol. 2 (New York: Atheneum, 1970) 68.

[48]Karl Vossler to Rector, 26 April 1926 (University of Munich, Vossler file, E-130 IV Bu 756).

[49]Protocols for the Senate meeting, University of Munich, 13 November 1926.

colleagues, in a eulogy at Vossler's funeral more than thirty years later, cited it as an example of his "high courage."[50]

Vossler also had to deal with the Student Corporations concerning their participation in the Jubilee festivities, and here he showed himself strongly opposed to the anti-Semitism of so many German Nationalists. He asked the students to allow the Corporations that admitted Jews to participate, along with other Corporations, in the events celebrating the Jubilee.[51] In this effort he was successful, an achievement rewarded a headline in the Nazi newspaper: "An Unworthy Rector."[52] Vossler illustrated in his personal stance, more strongly perhaps than any other individual professor of that time, the way in which an aristocrat, an elitist in many ways, a scholar in the truest and best sense could adapt to the role of educator in a democracy. He recognized the impact of the nonverbal communications students were receiving from their faculties—symbols, celebrations, club affiliations—and he wanted his colleagues to join him in helping the students clarify the meaning of such things in their own experience. He made the point to the professors that while flying a flag might look like a small thing, the decision about whether to fly it or not was not a small thing.

The inability and/or unwillingness on the part of the academic community to hear this kind of warning about the consequences of their refusal to accept the Republic is one of the key factors in explaining the ease with which the universities adapted to the Third Reich. An Adolf Hitler did not underestimate the importance of symbols and role models. Unlike Dr. Luther's bewilderment of 12 May 1926 at the stir caused by his instruction to the embassies to fly the black-red-white, Hitler's studied use of symbols caused him to have a presidential decree issued on 12 March 1933, immediately after his appointment, abolishing the black-red-gold flag and prescribing the black-red-white of the Reich. Bismarck's flag would fly side by side with the swastika. What did this say to the universities?

One answer came loud and clear. The pro-rector at Heidelberg, Professor Otto Ermannsdorffer, rejoiced in the "restoration" of the flag:

> Just as the old black-red-white flag and the banner of the new Germany [swastika] wave together over our celebration, so should the university of the future

---

[50]Aloys Wenzl, "Erinnerungen aus der Geschichte der Letzen 50 Jahre Unserer Universität," in *Jahrbuch der Ludwig-Maximilians Universität, 1957-1958*, 57.

[51]Karl Vossler, "To the Student Corporations" (December 1926) *MU #8*.

[52]*Völkischer Beobachter*, 2 March 1927. See also references to him 6/7 February and 26 July 1927.

be built on the best and most vital living tradition of the glorious German past
in organic union with the idea of the national will to renewal.[53]

The demise of the Weimar Republic was no more regretted by the professors
than was the loss of its flag. By linking the swastika with the old imperial symbol, they saluted the resurgence of their beloved nationalism in the new State,
one that would have a Reich, a Führer, and a Kulturmission.

---

[53]Otto Erdmannsdorffer, "Reden zur Feier der Nationalien Erhebung," 1 March 1933,
HU #20. "Pro-rector" was the title given to the one who was rector the year before.

Chapter Three

The Unreformed University

The fact that the professors were stubbornly opposed to the Weimar Republic and that they gave strong witness in their writings and speeches to a German Nationalist bias may only identify them as middle and upper German bourgeoisie of the 1920s. The following questions should engender wider speculation: "Should there not have been a qualitative difference in their political perceptiveness because they were university professors?" and "Should not educators assume additional responsibilities toward the common good of the society in which they exist?" "Were the Weimar universities a microcosm within which the alienation and divisiveness of the Republic were mirrored?"

In the various works done on the resistance movements against National Socialism, whether focused on the army, the church, labor unions, or the foreign office, historians emphasize the particular institutional structures within which individuals came to their decisions to oppose the Hitler regime. In an effort to make a fair judgment of what was involved in resistance, most writers acknowledge the tightness or looseness of the bureaucratic organization that restricted the individual or permitted him to risk opposition.[1] In the attempt to understand why resistance did *not* occur in the universities, it may be equally important to look at the structures. Initially, one might think that the university—more than the church, the army, or the foreign office—was a place of great freedom. A closer examination reveals, however, that such was not the case.

I turn, then, to an examination of the context within which the professors worked at the Weimar universities: What was the organizational structure? Who were the students? Where was the locus of power? What were the operational values of the academic community? What did the announced goal of educa-

---

[1] See *Central European History* 4 (December 1981) for several articles on the resistance. Essential to the one by Leonidas E. Hill, "A New History of Resistance to Hitler," is the question of criteria used in determining who was a "resister."

tion—*Bildung*—have to say about citizenship? How did the internal decision-making process relate to life in a democracy?

In order to achieve some insight into the university's self-understanding in the years 1925-1933, I shall examine the organizational structures and governance, including their relations to the *Lände* in which they existed as well as their internal procedures for making decisions. In addition, I must explore the nature of the student bodies of that period, their expectations and qualifications, and the role assigned to them within university governance. Next, I shall examine the curricula of the Weimar period, seeking to understand and criticize it by reference to the European tradition out of which it came. Finally, because I am assessing the role played by the professors in preparing the German people for National Socialism, I shall review their philosophy of education insofar as it has relevance to the outcome of their educational efforts.

Once having developed a sort of "typical" Weimar university, it should be possible to understand some of the proposals for reform. From the many diverse suggestions for change, I will cover only two: that of Carl Becker, who was Prussian Minister of Culture and Education and whose viewpoint was one of immediate practical necessity, and that of Max Scheler who, as a philosopher, dealt with the more theoretical aspects of the question.

In retrospect, it is known that neither their proposals for reform, nor those offered by any other persons, were accepted by the faculties. The universities, therefore, remained "unreformed."

I

In 1925 the universities in Germany were still organized according to the traditional model of European institutions.[2] From the founding of universities in Paris and Bologna, on through the founding of Prague, Heidelberg, Tübingen, and Ingolstadt (later Munich), universities were basically corporations of scholars and teachers. Faculties were identified according to the three main professions for which the students were being trained: law, medicine, and theology. The "Masters" governed the internal life of the university and carried on whatever business needed to be conducted with the local civic officials.

---

[2]For a general history of early universities, see Hastings Rashdall, *The Universities of Europe in the Middle Ages*, 2 vols. (Oxford: The Clarendon Press, 1936). An interesting aspect of university history is dealt with in John W. Baldwin and Richard Goldwaite, eds., *Universities in Politics* (Baltimore: Johns Hopkins University Press, 1972). Regarding the German universities, see Gerhard Hess, *Die deutsche Universität, 1930-1970* (Bad Godesberg: Inter Nationes, 1968), and Michael Doberl, ed., *Das Akademische Deutschland*, 4 vols. (Berlin: C. A. Weller, 1930-1931).

As the governing role of the States (*Lände*) increased, the locus of significant relationship with political authority shifted to that level. In 1794 Prussia decreed that all its universities were to be "State" institutions and the professors would be designated as civil servants. During the next decade the king of Prussia made it clear that he regarded the major task of the university to be the training of men for government service within a context of strong Protestant orthodoxy. But this did not alter the fundamental respect that the State was to show in regard to the faculties' power over the curricula and other internal affairs.

When the University of Berlin was founded (1810), this same identification was given it as a corporation of faculties. It followed the normal organization into faculties of law, medicine, and theology, but added a new faculty, that of philosophy. Wilhelm von Humboldt, as the Prussian Minister of Education and Culture, was placed in charge of the new university, and he made it clear from the beginning that there were to be no sectarian restraints on academic freedom. The State would respect the faculties' right to "freedom for teaching" and "freedom for learning."[3]

The pattern, therefore, that was handed on from the early universities was given new and official State recognition in the nineteenth century. The autonomy of the academic community, often a problem in the town/gown controversies over many centuries, was never surrendered to civil authority, but the faculties did recognize the legitimate interests of the civic community in the life and activities of the universities. As a whole, the German people held their universities in high regard and were in agreement with the policy of State support and respect for their freedom.[4]

However, when one speaks of the "academic community" and its autonomy, that phrase refers only to a small segment of the community—about twenty-six percent of the faculties at Berlin, Munich, and Heidelburg in 1930.[5] It refers, of course, to *Ordentlicher Professoren* (full professors). The rest of the teachers were called *Ausserordentlicher* or *Nichtordentlicher*—what is termed today assistant or associate professors. Finally, there were the *Dozenten*, lecturers with permission to teach on a kind of ad hoc basis, with no appointment and no salary. They were allowed to collect fees from the students for the particular lectures they gave.

---

[3]Paul R. Sweet, *Wilhelm von Humboldt: A Biography*, 2 vols. (Columbus: Ohio State University Press, 1980) 1:53-57.

[4]Fritz K. Ringer, *The Decline of the German Mandarins* (Cambridge MA: Harvard University Press, 1969) 35-38.

[5]Ibid., 77.

It was the customary practice for the full professors to constitute the Senate, to elect the rector and the deans, to nominate persons for the professorships as they became available, and to make all decisions regarding curricula and student discipline. By the late 1920s Munich, Tübingen, and Heidelberg all had, in addition to this Senate (which was now called the Small Senate), a Large Senate in which the other teachers had representation; its powers were limited to student discipline and a few other relatively unimportant internal matters.[6] The Small Senate dealt with the Ministry of Culture and Education. It had the power to accept or resist all proposed reforms and so determined the role that the university played in the life of the wider society. Members of the Small Senate exerted control over faculty appointments. It was their prerogative to draw up a list of three nominees for an available post and to submit that list to the Ministry for final selection. Generally, there was a mutuality of interests between the university and the *Landtag* so that the appointments were based on the judgment of the professors. However, in those *Lände* where, during the Weimar period, the Ministries were more "democratic," there were some tensions. The nominees were usually of the same mind-set as their patrons on the faculties (German Nationalist) and so, unless the minister was willing to be accused of "politics," he was hindered from changing the composition in the direction of Democrats or Socialists. Although a good number of Jewish men entered the ranks of *Dozenten* and were satisfactory lecturers, only a very small percentage found their way to the rank of professor. Once again, the "acceptable" kind of anti-Semitism, of which Speer spoke, seems to have been present.

The system of advancement was so slow that the average age of full professors was generally in the upper fifties. Many of the same men who dominated the scene in the days of imperial Germany were still occupants of prestigious chairs in the late 1920s. The junior faculty had organized in the first decade of the century into the *Nichtordinarienverbindung* for the purpose of making grievances known to the Ministry. However, their participation in governance remained minimal or nonexistent.

The composition of the faculties in the different universities was not static. It was customary for a professor to move from place to place, depending on the renown he achieved in his discipline and the "call" that came to him from another faculty. For professors, the result of this mobility was the absence of loyalty to a particular university or faculty and a closer affiliation with others in their disci-

---

[6]In addition to the general works on the German universities mentioned above, I have used the constitutions of the universities at Munich, Heidelberg, and Tübingen as well as the protocols of the Senate meetings.

plines than with colleagues at the university itself. The fact that they were civil servants and their salaries were determined by the State meant that professors had little reason for choosing one university rather than another in terms of personal living. It also meant that one of the topics—faculty salaries—that has so often been a unifying topic at American faculty meetings was argued in a different arena, that is, in the *Landtag*. In difficult economic times such as the early Weimar period, the professors tended to offer lectures to supplement their income, a situation that then left virtually nothing for the *Dozenten*.

An environment was thus created in which the social and economic status of younger teachers depended on extraneous factors: on the marriages they made, the inherited wealth they enjoyed, or the personal patronage of a master. Ringer has described the prewar atmosphere at most universities as "rank consciousness, favoritism, and mutual resentment"[7] among the various groups; the continuation of this ambiance at the time of the Republic is clear. Those who were in power cultivated the younger teachers, who were seen as "disciples," in the hope that they would carry on the master's work—but not so soon as to displace him. The sole criterion for the granting of the *venia legendi* (license to teach) was often the judgment of one professor, a situation that led to undue deference being paid to the elders. There was no mechanism for an authentic evaluation by one's peers.

In sum, the organizational structures of the university affirmed the status quo and severely limited the possibility for adaptation to new needs. Despite the many brilliant individuals who were professors at that time, the power structure led to mediocrity. It did not reward creative or innovative young teachers in the university, but rather kept them from influencing the educational process in any substantive way.

The second major component of a university is the students. The tradition of the universities in Europe had developed along the lines of Paris, where the governance was in the hands of the professors—the masters—rather than along the model of Bologna, where the students held the power, hired the faculties, and paid them their salaries. The structure of the Weimar universities allowed for no participation by the students. An exception to this was their presence in the Large Senate when cases regarding discipline were being heard. This lack of regard for student participation in governance was to bear undesirable fruit in the next decade. Gerhard Hess pointed out that Nazi propaganda owed some of its great success among the students to the fact that "the traditional German university is conceived of in relation only to the uppermost stratum of academic society, the Ordinary Professors."[8]

---

[7]Ringer, *The Decline*, 55.

[8]Hess, *Die deutsche Universität*, 18.

The new Weimar constitution, with its democratic form and proportional representation, was proposed by state educational authorities as a model for student governments in the university—the *Allgemeiner Studentischer Ausschuss* (AStA). However, because of the provision for proportional representation, the power within the AStAs was quickly seized by the fraternities, with a consequent repudiation of democratic principles. The AStAs had been formed to represent student needs to faculties and to the ministries, but they soon became political-action groups. In 1919 a national student organization was formed to unite the local councils and to deal with issues that transcended the individual university. Unfortunately, the *Deutsche Studentenschaft* was captured by right-wing forces by 1924. Their great cause became the inclusion of all German students—whether within the Weimar Republic or in the lands no longer part of Germany—in the national organization. Since the Austrian units were highly anti-Semitic, this move to include them had a divisive effect on the campuses and made further collaboration between the students and the Weimar ministers impossible. Steinberg makes a telling point about the role of the faculties in all this.

> Student democratic institutions were never implanted with the seeds of real life. While a lack of clear definition of the prerogatives of student government in a different setting would have permitted students to develop their responsibilities in creative directions, the German faculties were indifferent, if not hostile, to the new phenomenon. Instead, the universities encouraged the traditional fraternities which continued to represent student bodies on ceremonial occasions.[9]

In the period being studied (1925-1933), the composition of the student bodies was still largely upper middle class; twenty-three percent of them had fathers who had gone to universities. Statistics indicate that only about four percent of the male students and one and two-tenths percent of the females in 1928 could be considered "lower class." These percentages are even more significant when one notes the enormous increase in the number of university students that had occurred after World War I. Whereas in 1914 Germany had a population of 67,100,000 and a university enrollment of 61,000, after the war the population had decreased to 59,300,000 (because of the loss of both territory and population), but the number of university students was up to 72,000. By 1931 there were 95,780.[10]

---

[9]Michael Stephen Steinberg, *Sabers and Brown Shirts* (Chicago: University of Chicago Press, 1977) 61.

[10]Various works that I used on the students give different data based on different sources and different definitions of a university (some include the technical institutes and others do not). I have used the population figures from the *Encyclopedia Britannica*

This increase was due, in large part, to the policies of the Weimar government. When the Constitution had been written, the questions of education were seen as very important for the new Republic. Article 146 called upon the new government to pass a national law that would provide uniformity in the various *Lände* with regard to the lower schools. A "Basic School Law" was passed on 28 April 1920 and it prescribed a four-year common primary school for all. Already there had been pressure to accept a greater variety of educational experiences as admission credentials for the university, and in some cases this had been done. However, it was only with the greatest reluctance that the professors agreed to accept anything other than the traditional diploma—the *Abitur*—since they believed strongly in the classical education of the *Gymnasium*, which it represented. Now this same diploma could be awarded by other types of secondary schools, and the university was required to admit anyone possessing it.[11]

It does not take much imagination to visualize the crowded classrooms and lecture halls, the inadequate libraries and laboratories that resulted from this new wave of students in the 1920s. Given the strain on its financial resources, the government did not have the needed capital for new buildings. Three new universities had come on the scene: Frankfurt (1914), Hamburg (1919), and Cologne (1919), but they provided relatively little relief. In 1930, after ten years of steady growth, the small university at Tübingen reported that 1,000 of its 3,300 students had been added in the preceding five years. The Minister of Culture and Education for Württemberg, in detailing this situation to the *Landtag*, pointed out that the number of *Abiturs* awarded in that State from 1925 to 1930 had increased from an average of 847 a year to 1,438.[12] The minister pointed out that while the university was obliged to admit all these students—since they had the *Abitur*—no provision had been made by the *Landtag* for increased financial support. He blamed the very high number of applications on the equally high rate of unemployment and was of the opinion that

---

(Chicago: William Benton, 1971) 10:344, and taken the percentages from Ringer, *The Decline*, 65. Konrad Jarausch, *Students, Society and Politics* is the best analysis and presentation of the data that I have found for the English-speaking audience. He describes the postwar boom in enrollment as followed by a slight decline in the years 1924-1929 because of an improved economy and greater stability in Weimar. Renewed unemployment resulting from the worldwide depression pushed enrollments up again in 1930-1931 (pp. 419-20).

[11]Ringer, *The Decline*, 67-72.

[12]Kultusminister to Staatsminister, 15 February 1930 (Württembergisches Staatsarchiv, Stuttgart) E. 130. 55. Apparently, Tübingen's increase did not fluctuate as much as some of the others.

many persons were coming to study simply because they could not find work. Similar complaints were made at Heidelberg and Munich: too many students, many not adequately prepared for the traditional university curriculum, and too few financial resources to deal with them. Not surprisingly, the democratization of the lower schools—promoted by Weimar—was blamed for the intellectual weaknesses of those now possessing the *Abitur*.

In addition to the sheer numbers problem, the German faculties had to deal with the mobility of their students. Like their professors, students had the freedom to go to any university and to study under any professor. As a result, they also—like their teachers—did not identify with a particular institution and often spent their semesters at several different universities. One was not a "Munich man" in the same way that one's contemporaries might be "Harvard men" or "Oxford men," and this may have contributed to the lack of interest in student government within the university. It was, rather, across university lines that the students had organized in 1919 into the *Deutsche Studentenschaft* for the purpose of keeping their financial needs before the legislatures and ministries. These needs were very real even after the economy began to pick up in the last half of the decade and many students had the new—to them— experience of working while studying.

Naturally, the picture of the "typical" German university student is hard to draw with scientific accuracy because of the great variety among the universities themselves. In addition, many of the statistical studies include technical institutes among universities while others do not. The most-complete collection and analysis of the relevant data about the students has probably been done by Steinberg and Jarusch. Steinberg concludes that despite the numerical increase in students from middle-class homes, the cultural tone of the universities remained that of the "old elite."[13]

Student lives in the 1920s were not yet touched by radio, telephone, TV, or the Volkswagen—all potential scapegoats for students' lack of commitment to the rigors of the intellectual life. But they did attend operas and plays, go out drinking together, and sometimes ended by dueling. For the promotion of such "good fellowship" there were the *Corps* (fraternities), open only to male students and winning the active support of about fifty percent of them.[14] With centuries of ritual and tradition behind them, the *Corps* displayed their caps

---

[13]Steinberg, *Sabers and Brown Shirts*, 35-36.

[14]There is disagreement about the percentage of German students who were members of the *Corps* and about their strength and importance. See the charts in Steinberg, *Sabers and Brown Shirts*, 45-46. From all accounts they tended to be exclusive, in-bred, and nationalistic.

and colors, played a significant role in the university's patriotic celebrations, and provided an intergenerational experience because the *alte Herren* (former members) retained strong links with the current students. This camaraderie was one of the channels through which the nationalistic and anti-Semitic sentiments of one generation were handed on to another.

Unfortunately, neither the *Corps* nor the AStAs had the benefit of faculty guidance or supervision. What might have been seen as an opportunity for training in self-governance and responsible decision making, for leadership and community service—what we would call cocurricular education—was ignored. This lack of attention to the "whole person" was to have disastrous results when the National Socialist movement "coordinated" all student groups, promoting an exciting participation in the achievement of common goals. What had not been offered to them by their professors would be offered by the party.

II

The organizational structure, with its faculties of law, medicine, theology, and philosophy was a natural outgrowth of the need for professional training and was grounded in the belief that the foundation for all professions had been received in the studies of the traditional *Gymnasium*. Each university tended to specialize in one of the four faculties, and the reputation of the university acted as a magnet to the best professors in that field. It followed that students interested in that particular discipline came to that university to study under the master.

At the time of the founding of the University of Berlin in 1810, the faculties had strong representation by both philosophers and philologists.[15] While Wilhelm von Humboldt is credited with being the founder of this university, which would come to be a model for all others, he was surrounded by outstanding scholars: Johann Gottlieb Fichte, F. W. J. Schelling, Friedrich Hegel, F. E. D. Schleiermacher, and Friedrich von Schiller. Some of these men had been involved in the University of Jena's protest against what they regarded as too much State censorship; they firmly believed in the freedom to learn. The internal debates that accompanied the founding of the university led to a new faculty—philosophy—which was subdivided into languages, literature, history, and philosophy as one set and the natural sciences as the other. What they intended by this was an end to what they saw as the dominance of theology and law over philosophical thought.[16]

---

[15]John E. Craig, *Scholarship and Nation Building: The Universities of Strasbourg and Alsatian Society, 1870-1939* (Chicago: University of Chicago Press, 1984) 13-14; Sweet, *Humboldt*, 2:53-71.

[16]Sweet, *Humboldt*, 2:57.

With this addition, then, the universities remained satisfied. The courses listed for the years 1925-1933 were within the parameters of these faculties. Significantly absent are the social sciences: economics, sociology, political science, psychology as separate faculties. Ringer has explained the very complex reasons for the refusal of the German mandarins to recognize these studies as having distinctive content or methodology. Proposals to include them in the curriculum were occasionally labeled as "socialistic."[17] Outstanding work had been done in all these fields by German scholars in the late nineteenth and early twentieth centuries, but for the most part they had to work in "institutes" rather than in the universities. Franz Neumann had complained: "The study of social and political reality found virtually no place in German university life. Scholarship meant essentially two things: speculation and book learning. Thus what we call social and political science was largely carried on outside the universities."[18]

Students in the 1920s who were interested in studying such fields had to find courses in disparate faculties and choose them without any principle of integration. The relevant material was hidden in courses offered by the law faculty, the philosophy faculty, or the theology faculty. The only psychology available was in the faculty of medicine and the only economics was political economy.[19]

As a result of this aversion to the social scientists, the professors isolated them in the institutes and it was there, rather than in the universities, that important discussions took place about the impact of modern society on human life. The university, with its theology and philosophy faculties, should have been the forum for debating the new sociological theories about community, race, nation, and state. On the contrary, the cross-fertilization of ideas was dreaded rather than welcomed, and this by a community that saw itself as the guardian of culture. Such fear on the part of the professors led them to preclude reflection on the political and social dimensions of modern economic and industrial developments at the very time when such realities were influencing the direction of their own country and the world to an unprecedented degree.

The curricula of the universities thus remained unreformed. The professors failed to see how their rigidity hampered the integration of knowledge that could be gained from the study of different disciplines as they interacted in

---

[17]Regarding the efforts to introduce the social sciences, see Ringer, *The Decline*, 143-80 and 228-41.

[18]Franz Neumann, *The Social Sciences*, as quoted in Peter Gay, *Weimar Culture: The Outsider as Insider* (New York: Harper and Row, 1968) 38.

[19]According to Ringer, social scientists "did their scholarly work in an atmosphere of extraordinary tension and instability" (*The Decline*, 227).

confronting social questions. They refused to make the very contribution that one might legitimately have expected from the academic community.

III

The professors' defense was that it was not within their scholarly competence to deal with such questions. Their responsibility was to be faithful to their mission of cherishing *Kultur* and thus to give an education that would result in the "cultivated person"—*Bildung*. This is the vocabulary that appears with regularity in the writings and speeches of the late 1920s and early 1930s. They speak constantly of the "whole person" who is the object of *Bildung*, the need for synthesis of knowledge, and the outcome to be hoped for—that the youth will become the culture-bearers for the future. The language they use is the language of Humboldt and Fichte,[20] but the intervening century, with its industrialization and its wars, made the language anachronistic. It needed to take account of new realities and new understandings.

It is important to recall some of Fichte's educational philosophy, to hear his words as spoken and written in his own time, and then to hear them being used in the 1920s. When Fichte and Humboldt began their work at the University of Berlin in 1810, they took a strong position on individual human rights and focused on the defense of the university's "freedom" against undue interference by the State. At the same time, they saw their mission as one of preparing men for government service and thus for service to society; these goals did not seem to contradict their plea for autonomy because the person to be sought through education was the "cultivated person." Even prior to Berlin, the goal had been stated by the University of Göttingen as "the full and harmonious training of the whole individual, the forming of aesthetically pleasing 'cultivated' personalities . . . to transform the learner's whole character, to make him a new man."[21] This was *Bildung*. The same desire to affect the "whole" person was expressed by Humboldt when he said: "Knowledge alone, which comes from and can be planted in the depths of spirit, also transforms character, and for the state, just as for humanity, facts and discourse matter less than character and behavior."[22]

---

[20]In addition to Ringer's interpretation of Fichte, I have found useful H. S. Reiss, ed., *The Political Thought of the German Romantics, 1793-1815* (Oxford: Blackwell, 1955) and Reinhold Aris, *History of Political Thought in Germany, 1789-1815* (New York: Russell & Russell, 1965) 345-60.

[21]Ringer, *The Decline*, 19.

[22]Daniel Fallon, *The German University* (Boulder CO: Associated University Press, 1980) 25. The quotation is from Humboldt's "Über die innere und aussere Organization der bisheren wissenschaftlichen Anstalten zu Berlin."

In his famous *Addresses to the German Nation* (1808), Fichte had articulated his own philosophy of education, which similarly stressed the interaction of intellectual training and service to the community. Fichte envisioned "a place of learning [the university] where all reference to an extraneous aim was excluded and where a deep and unified study of philosophy would be the core of a broadly humanistic curriculum."[23] Since he believed that all knowledge was essentially "one," he insisted that all other branches of learning could be and should be subjected to the free, rational critique that a single system of philosophy could give. This was a logical corollary to his notion of free inquiry, which had been already developed in his *Critique of All Revelation* (1792), but now it was related to the function of the university itself. It was for this reason that he argued so strongly for a separate faculty of philosophy and made it a cornerstone at Berlin.

Fichte saw a bond between philosophic training and the individual person's appreciation of freedom: "Education for clarity means education for freedom."[24] One hears echoes of Plato in Fichte's suggestion that there should be a Republic of Scholars charged with the selection of the ruler for the State and in his assumption that men trained in philosophic modes of thought will be the best fitted to make wise decisions for society. Through the university—it was argued by those who stressed the role of philosophy—society will thus "raise and purify the German spirit until it becomes a pure embodiment of humanity."[25]

The University of Berlin, then, was envisioned as a place where the "art of learning" was to be the sole object. Society should not expect the university to assume the burden of professional training, but should welcome its dedication to the single task of cultivating the "things of the mind." But again Fichte stresses the link between this kind of education and the individual's freedom, which will make him a valuable member of the community. Speaking to the youth of Germany, he said: "Believe in your freedom and you are free—create, shape, and form the things of the outside world according to your ideas and aims and you are their master and they must serve you, your destiny is to be

---

[23]Johann Gottlieb Fichte, *Addresses to the German Nation* (New York: Harper and Row, 1968).

[24]Reiss, *The Political Thought*, 124.

[25]Martin Doerne, "Problems of the German University," in Walter M. Kotschnig and Elined Prys, eds., *The University in a Changing World* (Freeport NY: Books for Libraries Press, 1932) 56.

master and theirs is to serve."[26] "Things of the mind" is not synonymous with "reason," but rather opposed to it. Fichte rejected the great god of the Enlightenment—reason—as a sterile thing. To him, as to German classicists, the "things of the mind" embraced the riches of human experience as preserved in the masterpieces of Greek and Roman literature, philosophy and art. Exposure to these ideas would impart the kind of education desired; it would produce "free men" who would understand their "social responsibility" and would build a German nation that rested on the "autonomy of man as its most important ethical principle." Ethics and politics were thus related to one's intellectual development and constituted a "humanistic" education.

From this concept of the cultivated person as the free person, it was not hard to move to Fichte's understanding of a "religious" duty to live "for the species," defined as community. Far from decrying political concern, Fichte in his *Addresses to the German Nation* exhorted his fellow countrymen to strengthen their intellectual achievements as the best way of aiding their nation.

For those who read Fichte, such statements are almost self-evident. In the Judeo-Christian tradition of Western Europe the search for truth was always to be inspired by love and ordained toward service.[27] But what distinguishes

---

[26]Aris, *History of Political Thought,* 116. It is interesting to note that this relationship between a liberal education and freedom was also at the heart of John Henry Newman's philosophy of education. In his classic work, *The Idea of a University* (New York: Doubleday Image, 1959) 129, he states: "He [the student] apprehends the great outlines of knowledge, the principles on which it rests, the scale of its parts, its lights and its shades, its great points and its little, as he otherwise cannot apprehend them. Hence it is that his education is called 'liberal.' A habit of mind is formed which lasts through life, of which the attributes are freedom, equitableness, calmness, moderation, and wisdom: or what in former discourse I have ventured to call a philosophical habit."

An interesting study has been done by U. Gopalakrishnaiah entitled *A Comparative Study of the Educational Philosophies of J. G. Fichte and J. H. Newman* (Waltair: Andhra University Press, 1973). I find myself in disagreement with one distinction the author makes between the thought of the two men, namely that Fichte saw education as oriented toward society whereas Newman saw it only in terms of the benefit to the individual. The quotation from Newman given in the following footnote would support a different view.

[27]One sees this expressed in Newman, *The Idea,* 434. In speaking to the young men of Dublin, Newman said: "I do not desire this benefit [university education] to you, simply for your own sakes. For your own sakes certainly I wish it, but not on your account only. Man is not born for himself alone. . . . You were born for Ireland, and, in your advancement, Ireland is advanced—in your advancement in what is good, and what is true, in knowledge, in learning, in cultivation of mind, in enlightened attachment to your religion, in good name and respectability and social influence, I am contemplating the honour and renown, the literary and scientific aggrandizement, the increase of political power, of the Island of the saints."

Fichte's line of reasoning is that he moves from this rather broad notion of community to the very precise entity of the State. In his own day this meant the "nation," the cultural unity of the people. "Germany" did not yet exist as a nation-state, but it was to Fichte the word that meant homeland, people, and community—and this he denoted as *Kulturstaat*. It was of the German people that he spoke, regardless of their present geographical boundaries or ruling house; it was to the people (*Volk*) in its political form that the university must hand on the *Kultur* of which it is mentor. In doing so, it acts through those whom it has educated. To them an appreciation of the *Kultur* has been given; they must contribute what they have received to the life of the State, which is the bearer of that *Kultur*, or the *Kulturstaat*.

There are, of course, difficulties inherent in such a concept. Translated into another epoch or another political order, such a notion of bearing the culture forward would be used to support goals of political and imperial aggrandizement. The young men to whom Fichte was speaking in 1811 were succeeded ultimately by the foot soldiers of World War I at Langemarck. Germany's dedication to her special *Kulturmission* was to have serious consequences probably not foreseen by Fichte.

What was it that happened to the concept of *Kulturstaat* in the years that lay between Fichte and the Weimar Republic? Fichte had seen freedom and unity as complementary aspects of the community, but the effort to unify Germany politically in the last half of the nineteenth century brought with it curtailment of freedom, with regard both to individuals and to the various *Lände*. Restrictive measures such as the *Kulturkampf* created lasting tensions among groups within the one "nation." Industrialization also tended to divide classes and regions, thus creating another impediment to unity. When pressed to make a choice between freedom and unity, the professors tended to go with an authoritarian leader such as Bismarck and to hope that under his leadership the true strength of the "nation" would revive.

The second half of the nineteenth century also witnessed a repudiation, in practice, of Fichte's dedication to the "cultivation of the things of the mind"— that is, a broad concern for human values and ethical norms discoverable through a study of the tradition. New currents of thought led to the imposition of the "scientific method" on all disciplines in such a way that *Wissenschaft* (pure science) came to mean narrow specialization and reliance on positivistic criteria for all intellectual endeavors. Critical thinking, as the fruit of general "cultivation," gave way to precise analytical modes of scholarly research to such an extent that the gap between the university and the average citizen widened and deepened.[28] When one adds to this the currents of Romanticism, with their stress on individualism and personality, one discovers why the link Fichte saw between freedom and unity was broken. No longer did the terms mean the same thing. The anti-intellectualism of the Romantics—such as the Conservative Revolutionaries—weakened society's traditional confidence in the universities and called for a new articulation of their mission. The original broad understanding of *Wissenschaft* as a philosophy of learning was smothered in the development of loyalties to the various academic disciplines, each of which had become *eine Wissenschaft*.[29] Historians clung to the notion of theirs as a humanistic discipline even while they adopted scientific methodology. Hence although the university professors continued to insist that they favored a philosophical kind of education, one that dealt with the "whole man," each professor lived within the confines of his own discipline, and any attempt at interdisciplinary programs was resisted. With few exceptions, the professorial class of 1890—even more so in 1925—could be described as a *Wissenschaftlich* island in the midst of a newly industrialized world, without point of contact and even perhaps without point of reference.[30]

Fritz Stern regards the late nineteenth century as a period in which the universities became "illiberal."[31] Fritz Ringer considers it the time of the "decline" of the "German Mandarins" in which the professors, like the Chinese Mandarins, held on to status and prestige, considered themselves the elite protectors of the intellectual heritage of their people, and disdained all involvement with the societal changes going on around them.[32] In response to what they perceived as a lack of meaning in industrialized society, they proposed a renewed emphasis on learning; hence they tried to link *Wissenschaft* and *Weltanschauung*.

---

[28]Regarding the many understandings of *Wissenschaft* and its relation to *Bildung*, see Ringer, *The Decline*, 253-434. These chapters need to be read and pondered since they deal with the fundamental questions of culture, knowledge, and education in twentieth-century Germany, in the midst of which the professors seemed to become incapable of clear decision.

[29]Ringer, *The Decline*, 102-103.

[30]One author describes them as "men . . . who disdained an active role in political affairs in order to devote undivided attention to their specialized academic disciplines." Douglas Tobler, "German Historians and the Weimar Republic" (Ph.D. dissertation, University of Kansas, 1967) intro.

[31]Fritz Stern, *The Failure of Illiberalism* (New York: Knopf, 1972).

[32]Ringer, *The Decline*, 129.

The search for the latter provides a key to the experience of the German people in the twentieth century. Although it means literally a "world view," it has overtones of a unifying philosophic position that brings wholeness to the way a person grasps reality. Ringer defines *Weltanschauung* as "the spiritual man's right of citizenship in the world of *Geist* (spirit) and therefore the justification of his dominion over the sensible world. It enables man, even without detailed specialized information, to understand the meaning and value of the several areas of human endeavor."[33] The university's self-understanding may well have been blurred at this point by the numerous and confusing new currents of learning. In literary circles outside the university there was the "search for meaning" that I have described in writing of the Conservative Revolutionaries. New schools of biblical criticism, the historicist movement among the historians, the new scientific vistas opened by Max Planck and Albert Einstein—all were forces to contend with. The new disciplines of sociology, psychology, and economics were insisting that there were other ways to go about learning. Given this explosion of knowledge and the ways of knowing, could the university still make a clear statement as to its purpose? Could it have articulated a connection between the love of learning and the day-to-day meaning that people find in life? Was the search for "wholeness" inevitably bound to disintegrate in the face of specialized knowledge?

The professors themselves seemed aware of the problem. In some rather heavy-handed analogies, they attempted to show how scientific learning could give insight into social, economic, or political life. What had been learned in psychology about the nature of guilt was utilized as a means of addressing, once more, the injustice of the "war-guilt lie."[34] A study of the life cycle of insects became a tool for understanding the necessity of specialization in modern life.[35] The professors gave the impression of a real, albeit pathetic, struggle to be relevant to their times. They seemed caught in a current swirling about them, one that threatened their very raison d'être.

Every discipline was splintered by the various currents of new thought and reflected the absence of synthesis. It was common to voice concern for the "whole person" and to seek to construct a symphony in which the differences of tone would be reconciled.[36] It was fashionable to point out that Germany

---

[33]Ibid., 104.

[34]Oswald Bumke, "Die Grenzen der geistigen Gesundheit," 28 June 1929, *MU* #16.

[35]Reinhard Demoll, "Über den Instinkt," *MU* #25 (1932).

[36]Ringer writes: "Biologists and physicians meant to study the *whole* organism; pedagogues and psychologists, the *whole* man. In sociology and in economics, it was the *whole* community. In every discipline, scholars made war upon individualism, naturalism, mechanism, and the like" (*The Decline*, 387). The whole section on "The Synthesis Movement" demonstrates this point; see 384-403.

had lost her "soul." The mandarins tried to reaffirm faith in the individual, but to do so in virtue of his membership in the community, where he would fulfill a function related to the whole. What was sought was a "reintegration of scholarship, cultivation and *Weltanschauung*."[37]

In reading the speeches and writings of the Weimar professors, one also gets a picture of the university by negation. Obviously, there was a lack of integration, of synthesis, of "symphony." It was a perfect vacuum into which there would come the call to a revitalized *Weltanschauung*. Yet there was a danger in using the university to produce such a cultural synthesis, for it might well interfere with the independence of thought so prized by the scholar. Men such as Friedrich Meinecke, Karl Vossler, Ernst Troeltsch, Karl Jaspers, Max Weber, and Ferdinand Tonnies voiced concern about an overly simple reduction of complex matters in order to achieve "wholeness." In fact, it was this very element in the work of the Conservative Revolutionaries that denigrated the intellectual mission of the university and tended toward an irrational and emotional appreciation of the Germanic *Kultur*. Deliberate efforts to have young people commit themselves to the promotion of a particular *Weltanschauung* were viewed with some alarm by these critics within the mainstream professoriat.

Karl Vossler went back to Fichte's view that such moral commitment must only come as a result—and an indirect one—of the intellectual training that was the true mission of the institution. He insisted, "The character and the will are only indirectly trained at the university, only through the exercise of the mind, the judgment of the critical faculties, and of comprehending reason. The independence and responsibility of thought remains our . . . most important goal."[38] In 1927 Vossler again emphasized this point in his inaugural address ("Politics and the Intellectual Life") as rector of the University of Munich. He insisted that the kind of politics that belonged in the university was the kind inherent in the development of prudent and wise men, the kind that attended to keenness of intellect and sharpness of judgment.[39] Max Weber had said something similar when he spoke in 1919 of the fact that only a special kind of politics belongs in the classroom.[40] Neither Weber nor Vossler argued for a view of the university that was indifferent toward the needs of society or the political structures that were developed to meet those needs; what the "modernist"

---

[37]Ibid., 392.

[38]Karl Vossler, "Die Universität als Bildungsstatte: Vortraggehalter am 15 December 1922" (München, 1923) 14.

[39]Karl Vossler, "Politik and Geistesleben," *MU* #8 (1927).

[40]Max Weber, *Politics as a Vocation* (Philadelphia: Fortress Press, 1965) passim.

professors did abhor was the use of the academic platform to develop a single
world view.

There was, then, a division within the academic community itself as to its
proper role vis-à-vis the political order. It had been easier for the "orthodox"
professors (who formed the majority) to articulate a relationship between university and state when they were operating within the Reich. They had much
more in common with the authoritarian and paternal structures of the prewar
State than with the new parliamentarianism which, to them, threatened the
Kulturstaat. The university's own internal governance contradicted the basic
democratic principles of Weimar. Perhaps most important, the new understanding of national unity as based on constitution and laws rather than on
"culture" was unacceptable. They feared that a democratization of the university would result in an academic institution analogous to the *Unrechtsstaat*.
Their resistance to changing anything within the university was nothing new.
In the late nineteenth century, more than 300 proposals for educational reform—many including higher education—had been submitted to the Prussian
Ministry of Education and Culture; none was enacted.[41]

The difficulty of reconciling the structures of university life, rigid and un-
changing, with the realities of political life was simply avoided by most of the
professors, as they gave themselves wholeheartedly to *Wissenschaft*.

A few persons—among whom were Eduard Spranger, Theodor Litt, Carl
Becker, and Max Scheler—proposed some reforms that might have brought
the universities into the mainstream, but none of their suggestions were
accepted.

IV

A closer look at the thought of two of these men, Carl Becker and Max
Scheler,[42] helps clarify the problem faced by the universities; the former ap-
proaches it as a practical matter while the latter deals with the issues from a
speculative point of view. It is important to recognize that the struggle took
place on both levels and was never resolved on either. Only with the Nazi
Gleichschaltung would the integration occur; ideology and movement would
meet and become one.

------

[41]Richard H. Samuel and R. Hinton Thomas, *Education and Society in Modern Germany* (Westport CT: Greenwood, 1971) 17.

[42]Regarding Becker, see *Carl Heinrich Becker, Ein Gedenkbuch* (Göttingen: Van-
denhoeck and Ruprecht, 1950) and Erich Wende, *C. H. Becker: Mensch und Politiker*
(Stuttgart: Deutsche Verlagsanstalt, 1959). Regarding Scheler, see John Raphael Staude,
Max Scheler (New York: The Free Press, 1967) and Manfred Frings, *Max Scheler*
(Pittsburgh: Duquesne University Press, 1965).

Carl Becker was Minister of Culture and Education in Prussia in 1921 and again from 1925 to 1930. His proposals for reform dealt with the actual institutional structures and practices that he felt were hindering a true education, one that would be relevant to life in a democracy. He urged the introduction of the social sciences into a curriculum that would allow them their own autonomy as disciplines. Becker also proposed interdisciplinary studies, a suggestion that caused him to be denounced by many of his colleagues as too "socialistic."[43] As early as 1919, when he worked with Konrad Haenisch in the Prussian Ministry of Education, Becker had supported the idea of revamping the governance structures in the universities and giving some rights to the junior faculty and students.[44] He favored self-government for the students because he believed that the universities had a responsibility to prepare the students for a leadership role in the new Republic.

Throughout Becker's time as minister he was opposed by most of the professors because they feared the effect of his proposed reforms on the traditional purposes of the university. As late as 1932 the Corporation of German Universities demanded that all German secondary schools remain strictly scholarly institutions.[45]

Not only was Becker rejected by the professors; he also suffered defeat at the hands of the students. His faith in their ability to make their own decisions if they had the necessary structure for self-government received a decisive blow in February of 1927. The Austrian students demanded the exclusion of Jewish students from the *Deutsche Studentenschaft* as a precondition for their own participation in it. Becker urged the Prussian students to resist and not to capitulate to this anti-Semitic demand. It was in that same year that Karl Vossler successfully pleaded with the student corporations at Munich to allow the Jewish students to participate in the Jubilee celebration.[46] Becker, however, was not as successful. The Prussian students rejected his position, and Becker was disillusioned: "The most beautiful dream of a wartime generation is over. Student self-government has come to an end."[47] While this may sound like a melodramatic reaction to one failure, it may mean that Becker felt little support from his colleagues in his efforts with the students.

---

[43]Ringer, *The Decline*, 228.

[44]Ibid., 70.

[45]Ibid., 77-78. This had been their consistent position in opposing innovations since the corporation was formed in 1920.

[46]Vossler, "Politik und Geistesleben," *MU* #8 (1927).

[47]Helmut Kuhn, ed., *Die deutsche Universität im Dritten Reich* (München: R. Piper & Co., 1966) 41.

Hess claims that Becker's resignation as minister in 1928, based at least partly on this defeat, marked the end of the possibility of meaningful reform in the universities.[48] Was it true that one person's efforts to swim against the tide of nationalism and anti-Semitism were so significant? What would the result have been if the group of professors who gathered in Weimar in 1926 under Meinecke's leadership had induced their colleagues to support Becker in this instance?

To what extent was latent anti-Semitism responsible for the lack of professorial support for Becker's position? We know that in the years 1926-1928 there was increasing denunciation of Jewish influence in the Weimar Republic and in cultural circles in Berlin; does this explain the speeches at the *Akademikertag* in 1927 calling for a halt to the appointment of Jews to the university faculties?[49] Was the response of the student corporations to the Austrian demand a reflection of their professors' views?

Ringer interprets the rejection of Becker's curricular reforms by the professors as the result of the self-satisfied image they had of themselves as defenders of academic standards. He says that such an image was certainly not unjustified; however, the trouble with it was that the professors failed to disentangle academic standards from "the whole complex of social prejudices that had grown up around the ideal of classical 'cultivation,'" thus leaving no room for a discussion of alternatives.[50] Alternative modes of education and of university governance would have required overcoming these social prejudices if the professors were to make it possible for all those with the ability and motivation for higher education to enjoy it. It would also have meant sharing their own power with colleagues who were younger and also with those of different political persuasion. Becker's reforms were too dangerous.

Another reformer of quite a different character was the philosopher Max Scheler. His career as a member of the university community was erratic and short-lived, due not to his scholarly opinions but to his many extramarital affairs, which made him a cause of scandal. He was forced to move from Munich to Jena, then to Bonn, and finally to Cologne. Whether or not his proposals for

---

[48]Hess, *Die deutsche Universität*, 8. It is interesting to note Becker's later influence on the educational reforms envisioned by the Kreisau circle of anti-Hitler resisters. According to Ger Van Roon, Becker had friends in that group, especially Peters and Reichwein. Moltke, the acknowledged leader of the Kreisau circle, mentioned him in a letter as early as September 1928. Ger Van Roon, *Neuordnung im Widerstand* (München: R. Oldenbourgh, 1967) 361n.

[49]Hans Peter Bleuel, *Deutschlands Bekenner Professoren zwischen Kaiserreich und Diktatur* (München: Scherz, 1968) 189.

[50]Ringer, *The Decline*, 78-79.

university reform would have received a more favorable hearing were it not for his moral lapses remains unknown, but it is worth pausing over them in order to recognize that to some persons the weaknesses in the university were obvious. Scheler was something of a gadfly among the new philosophical currents; he was close to such diverse personalities as Edmund Husserl, Max Weber, Adolf von Hildebrand (father of Dietrich), and Karl Muth (editor of the Catholic journal *Hochland*). Constantly open to new insights, he became known as one of the exponents of *Wissenssoziologie* (sociology of knowledge).

He identified five tasks for the university: handing on the tradition, development of it, research, cultivation of the person, and education for the community.[51] Although he was born of a Protestant father and a Jewish mother, Scheler had become a Catholic at the age of fourteen and in the years 1916-1922 he seems to have been most influenced by the Catholic tradition. He acquired an admiration for the Church's "community building power" and sought a way in which a similar force might be developed within the university.[52] In his critique of Eduard Spranger's *Das humanistische und das politische Bildungsideal im heutigen Deutschland* (1916), Scheler took issue with him on the subject of civic education. Tackling one of the most hotly debated questions of German academia at the turn of the century and on up into Weimar, Scheler objected to the directness of Spranger's approach.

> I would prefer, instead of the direct "civic education" which he advocates in order to develop the sense of State, a continual indication, pervading *all* relevant instruction, of how this or that literature, art, science, philosophy *fitted* into the State of the time . . . why certain groups of values stood outside, which features were conditioned by the nature of the social groups exhibiting them, and which *could* have arisen—given cultural potentialities latent in existing forces—but were frustrated by political conditions. To my mind, this indirect cultivation of the sense of State and community, constantly drawing attention to the fact that the highest fruits of the spirit are interdependent with political and social conditions, should renew the whole of thinking, in the direction of a deepened sense of State, much more intimately and permanently than any direct "civic instruction" geared to the State of the day. But the most important consideration is that the sense of State . . . should be attained, if at all, only as a particular formulation of an intensified sense of community.[53]

Unlike those who approached citizenship education as a prop for the *Kulturstaat*, Scheler returned to the Fichtean notion that the State receives its own

[51]Van Roon, *Neuordnung*, 361.

[52]Ernest W. Ranly, *Scheler's Phenomenology of Community* (The Hague: Martinus Nijhoff, 1966).

[53]Max Scheler, "The Reconstruction of European Culture," in *On the Eternal in Man*, tr. Bernard Noble (New York: Harper and Row, 1961) 426.

identity precisely because the culture, developed and protected a priori in the university, needs a "bearer." The State is thus the servant of the culture, as is the university, but it is the latter that decides what the State will embody. Scheler thus avoids the kind of civic education that would lead to the citizen's conformity to the State. Rather, he calls upon the academic community to exercise its own function precisely in criticizing the State according to the "values" that the professors have come to know and accept through their respective disciplines. Here he tended a bit toward the notion of "cultural synthesis," but he accompanied it with a caution against being caught up in the tide of popular movements and ideologies. Values were of paramount concern for Scheler; it is unfortunate that he was unable to produce a systematic treatment of the relationship he envisioned between the individual's value system and the life of the community.

According to one of his biographers, Scheler's inability to systematize his thought mirrored the cultural chaos of Weimar:

> [He] . . . provides an amalgam of several diverse intellectual currents. Here in his *Sociology of Knowledge*, as on earlier occasions, Scheler's mind, so receptive to diverse strains of thought—and so unconcerned with the incompatibility between these strains—serves as a microcosm of his intellectual milieu, of the culture of his epoch.[54]

Thus Scheler was himself unable to achieve the cultural synthesis he desired or to devise a system that would achieve his goal of making the intellectual tradition available to all classes of people. One of his proposals was to create two new types of academic institutions: a people's university to achieve his goal of popular learning, and a research institute for academics who would seek "synthesis" of the knowledge acquired in their various disciplines.[55] If Scheler had been able to develop his thought, in dialogue with some of the more orthodox professors, he might have been able to provide the conceptual link between their *Bildung* and his insight into the needs of society at large. Without such a satisfactory educational philosophy, the professors remained isolated in their self-understanding, rigid, rationalistic, and sterile.

In assessing the role played by the academic community in the crucial years before National Socialism, one finds that instead of paying attention to the need for reforms within the educational environment, the professors continued to look for extraneous causes of the cultural crisis they were enduring: the Weimar government, the Treaty of Versailles, the war-guilt lie, the stab-in-the-back, the inroads of cultural Bolshevism. The present form of the State was de-

---

[54]Staude, *Max Scheler*, 200.

[55]Ringer, *The Decline*, 281.

nounced as unworthy to be a "bearer" of the culture so dear to them; the profound chasm between culture as they conceived of it and civilization as a "relative" phenomenon with which they had to deal became only deeper. By resisting all efforts at reform—and, in fact, not even giving them a decent hearing—they increased the distance between university decision-making processes and parliamentary government. By dealing negatively with the newer disciplines of the social sciences, they clung to an outmoded context for human inquiry and guaranteed the irrelevance of their curricula. Not only did they fail to provide a satisfactory way of integrating learning and life, but they opened wide the doors to a movement that would provide a satisfying *Weltanschauung* of enormous consequences for Germany and for the world. The refusal to "let go" of many of their cherished social values led to their being "taken over" by the leaders of National Socialism.

Chapter Four

Unwelcome Dissent: Case Studies in Intolerance

The concept of academic freedom has generally demanded respect for a diversity of opinion within the university. It was one of the fundamental principles of Wilhelm von Humboldt in founding the University of Berlin, and from there it went out to influence nineteenth- and twentieth-century higher education in almost every part of the world. It demanded that the State not seek to use the universities as a way of assuring orthodoxy. It was seen as a necessary protection for the professors who, in their various disciplines, needed the freedom to pursue truth wherever it led them. One of the "glories" of German academic life was this guaranteed "freedom to teach" and "freedom to learn"; it is therefore somewhat surprising to discover a lack of tolerance within the university itself. It is difficult to accept the professors' claim to be "above politics" in terms of national political parties, given their record of discrimination against socialists, pacifists, and Jews at the time of the Weimar Republic.

These are the people whom Peter Gay identifies as "Outsiders" when he writes: "[German universities] were . . . nurseries of a wooly-minded militarist idealism and centers of resistance to the new in art or the social sciences; Jews, democrats, socialists, in a word outsiders, were kept from the sacred precincts of higher learning."[1] And Friedrich Meinecke narrowed it down even more; he complained that in the 1920s one had to be "German National" to get ahead in the university.[2]

It is an area of German university life where one finds portents of the prejudice and suppression of dissent that characterized the Third Reich. Indeed,

---

[1]Peter Gay, *Weimar Culture* (New York: Harper and Row, 1968) 3.

[2]Fritz K. Ringer, *The Decline of the German Mandarins* (Cambridge MA: Harvard University Press, 1969) 218.

the United States ambassador in Berlin made this point in 1936: "That the Nazis, however, are not to be entirely credited with the introduction of bigotry in German Universities but are perhaps only its more illustrious protagonists is proved by laws existing before the war forbidding any known Socialist from holding a teaching position."[3] The legal basis for the exclusion of socialists was found in the Lex Arons, a Prussian decree of 1899, by which instructors were brought under the disciplinary law of 1852. Leo Arons was a young physics *Dozent* at Berlin who was a known Social Democrat, sufficient cause for the State to withdraw his *venia legendi*. He was not accused of politicizing his classes, but he was denounced because "the deliberate promotion of Social Democratic purposes was . . . incompatible with a teaching post in a royal university."[4] Although a few of the professors at the university argued against this as a violation of academic freedom, the great majority in Berlin and elsewhere simply accepted the decision of the court that upheld the law.

Another case in which it was clear that nothing but a Nationalist position was acceptable was that of Veit Valentin, an instructor at Freiburg University in 1916.[5] His offense was in writing a critical review of a book by a Pan-Germanist. A professor at the university, Georg von Below, insisted that Valentin be disciplined if he would not voluntarily give up his *venia legendi*. Others on the faculty would not support a *Dozent* against a full professor.

There are several other well-known instances: Friedrich Wilhelm Forester, a pacifist at the University of Munich in the early 1920s;[6] Professor Bertold Maurenbrecher, attacked as a Marxist a decade later because he criticized

---

[3]Ambassador William Dodd to United States Department of State, 10 December 1936, #862.42/132.

[4]Richard H. Samuel and R. Hinton Thomas, *Education and Society in Modern Germany* (Westport CT: Greenwood Press, 1971) 117. See also Ringer, *The Decline*, 141-42.

[5]Ringer, *The Decline*, 56-57. Ringer refers to a detailed account of this case, but it was not available to the author: Felix Rochfal, ed., *Der Fall Valentin: Die amtlichen Urkunden* (München, 1920).

[6]File on Forester in University of Munich Archives. See also the account of his difficulty with Stresemann in Erich Eyck, *A History of the Weimar Republic*, 2 vols., trans. Harlan P. Hanson and Robert G. L. Waite (New York: Atheneum, 1970) 2:105. In a chronology that Emil Gumbel drew up for the Office of Strategic Services (USA) in New York in 1945 concerning the history of Bavaria, he notes that on 11 November 1918 Professor Friedrich Wilhelm Forester, a "well-known Catholic pacifist," was appointed ambassador from the Bavarian government to Switzerland. On 1 July 1919 he resigned, and in the same month the Bavarian Embassy in Berne was closed, presumably because of the new Weimar Republic. Gumbel Archives, Leo Baeck Institute, New York.

some of his colleagues for their nationalist opinions;[7] and Theodore Lessing of the University of Hanover because he made a disparaging remark about the "super-nationalism" of von Hindenburg during his campaign for the presidency in 1925. In the latter case, Lessing's colleagues themselves voted to exclude him from their faculty because he was no longer "worthy."[8]

Although various reasons are cited in these cases for the decision to exclude persons from the faculties, it is clear that the basic difficulty their colleagues had with them was that they were somehow "un-German." Recalling the obsession that the professors had with the *Kulturmission* and their responsibility to guard it against all outside forces, one can understand the logic of their position. Perceiving those who were different from themselves (German and Nationalistic) as not "worthy" of sharing in the noble mission of transmitting the traditional German values, they sympathized with laws and interpretations of law that permitted only narrow political horizons for those in academia. During the Weimar period the "democratic" officials in the Ministries of Education and Culture sometimes favored the appointment of persons favorably disposed to the Republic, but they received few, if any, nominations of such persons from the senates of the universities.

By the mid-1920s the right-wing students had become vocal opponents of any faculty members tainted with socialism or pacifism and, under the leadership of *Deutsche Studentenschaaft,* often led demonstrations against them. The role of the students was organized and effective in the case of Theodore Lessing.[9] By 1930 the leadership of the student movement was being taken over by the National Socialist student group (NSDStB) and, according to various studies of the student role in the burgeoning Nazi movement, they exercised great pressure within the universities. But the damage to academic freedom had been done long before that. Professors' basic attitude of intolerance toward their less-nationalistic colleagues at the universities unfortunately put them in the unenviable position of bedfellows with the radical NS students whom they despised for their vulgarity and street fighting. Although the professors might have preferred to ignore their colleagues who leaned toward socialism or pacifism or

---

[7]Anselm Faust, "Studenten und Nationalsozialistismus in der Weimarer Republik: Der Nationalsozialistische Deutsche Studentenbund" (dissertation, Ludwig-Maximilians-Universität, 1971) 355. This has since been published as *Der Nationalsozialistische Deutsche Studentenbund: Studenten und Nationalsozialismus in der Weimar Republik,* 2 vols. (Dusseldorf: Padagogischer Verlag Schwann, 1973).

[8]Hans Peter Bleuel, *Deutschlands Bekenner Professoren zwischen Kaiserreich und Diktatur* (München: Scherz, 1968) 157.

[9]Michael Stephen Steinberg, *Sabers and Brown Shirts* (Chicago: University of Chicago Press, 1977) 65.

who were Jewish, the insistence of the radical students that the universities be purged of all "un-German" elements pushed them to violate the very concept of academic freedom that they considered the hallmark of a true university. The strong nationalist bias of most of the professors made them powerless to stem the tide of a movement that so capitalized on the nationalist sentiments of the German people. It would soon be too late.

The charge of being un-German was fundamental in the exclusion of several faculty members during this period. To illustrate this point, and to help in assessing the role of the professors in such instances, there are two well-documented cases that arose at the universities of Munich, Heidelberg, and Tübingen. The first example is that of Emil Gumbel, who met with rejection at both Heidelberg and Tübingen[10]; the second, that of Hans Nawiasky at Munich. While there are several differences to be noted in the two cases, the root problem is the same, they were "unGerman" in their very persons (Jewish) as well as in their opinions (pacifism, socialism, internationalism). As such, they were unwelcome in academia.

I

Heidelberg was one of the earliest universities in Europe (1386), famed in song and story as a center of true learning and good fellowship. When it was reconstituted after the Napoleonic years, its constitution provided for two new faculties in addition to the traditional ones: social sciences and general studies. During the nineteenth century Heidelberg was known for its strong philosophy faculty, but as the twentieth century began, its social sciences, housed mainly in the *Institut für Sozial-und-Staatswissenschaften,* rivaled it. Here the influence of Max Weber had been strong. In the period before the war, he had

---

[10]Basic materials for the Gumbel case are from the Heidelberg University Archives 3, 5b, Nr. 332 (1930-1931) and 333 (1924-1925) and 431 (1925). Some materials are also located in the Tübingen University Archives and the Württembergisches Staatsarchiv. They are specified in the relevant footnotes as *HA, TA,* or *WS.* See also the work of Arye Zvi Carmon, "The University of Heidelberg and National Socialism" (dissertation, University of Wisconsin, 1974). The same basic story is told in Christian Jansen, "Der Fall Gumbel und die Heidelberger Universität, 1924-1932" (dissertation, University of Heidelberg, 1981). At present Dr. Jansen is working on a paper entitled "Heidelberger Professoren und Politik," for a commemorative book on the university's 600th anniversary in 1986, and an extensive dissertation on the Heidelberg professors active during 1914-1935.

While the few professors who supported Gumbel are identified as "democratic," there is no way of knowing the names of those on the other end of the spectrum. This is also the case with the listing of names from various universities in Herbert Döring, *Der Weimarer Kreis* (Meisenheim: Verlag Anton Hain, 1975); we know those who supported Weimar but not those whose political persuasion was German Nationalist.

gathered a group around him interested in exploring the new social and economic questions. Weber left for Munich after the war and died there very suddenly in 1920. His wife Marianne returned to Heidelberg and reconvened the group. It met off and on until 1944, although the participants changed. Some of the names connected with this Weber circle are: Emil Lederer, Gustav Radbruch, Karl Mannheim, Jacob Marschak, and Emil Gumbel.

Equally strong in Heidelberg during this period were the followers of Stefan George, a leading poet of the Conservative Revolution. His presence seems to have attracted many of the young academics, but it is hard to know if he had great political influence. The prevailing temper in Heidelberg, as well as in most university towns, was conservative and nationalistic; hence one does not come upon individual names on this end of the spectrum quite as easily if they were noted as socialistic or even democratic.

Some of the professors engaged in public debates and played some role in political parties. The names of Ludwig Curtius, Hermann Oncken, Alfred Weber, Gerhard Anschutz, and Gustav Radbruch are associated with such a forum where political issues were discussed from various points of view. According to Bleuel, "This form of understanding and tolerance and reasonable pragmatic thinking was alien to the German professors and before 1933 was possible only in the atmosphere of Heidelberg."[11]

Despite this image of openness, the Heidelberg faculty proved to be intolerant of dissenting voices when they belonged to one who was a mere *Dozent* and who held views out of step with the German Nationalist mind-set. I refer to the case of Emil Gumbel.

Gumbel was born in Munich in 1891, the son of a Jewish banker. He attended schools in Munich and Heidelberg and in 1923 began his teaching career at the *Institut für Sozial-und-Staatswissenschaften* as a lecturer in the field of statistics. Strongly influenced by an uncle who was a pacifist, Emil was a conscientious objector in World War I, remained a pacifist, and became a member of the Independent Socialist party (USPD). All of these characteristics would have been viewed by a majority of the professors as un-German, to say the least. But he had great promise as a mathematician and so they valued him as a lecturer. The "case" against him resulted from his activities outside the classroom rather than inside it.

On 26 July 1924 Gumbel gave an impromptu response to a speech on the question of war by retorting that since war was such a disgraceful thing, he did not think it proper to speak of those who died in it as having fallen "on a field

---

[11]Bleuel, *Deutschlands Bekenner*, 193. See also Carmon, "The University," 56-60.

of honor," but rather "on a field of dishonor."[12] When asked about his remarks later, he insisted that he was not imputing guilt to individuals, but rather to all of humanity because war still existed. He entitled his speech "War Never Again!"

His remarks were immediately protested by the German Nationalist People's Party, which saw in them a disparagement of German honor. The matter was referred to the University Senate and on 30 July Gumbel was suspended from lecturing, pending an investigation. On the first of August a committee was set up for this purpose; Professor Alexander Graf von Dohna was the chairman, and Professors Karl Jaspers and Baethgen were members. Despite Gumbel's defense—he meant that it was war that was dishonorable and not the German soldiers—the Senate notified him on 6 August that the philosophy faculty had passed a resolution to deprive him of his *venia legendi*. The reason given was that he had "attacked the human feelings of those who respect the men who fell in the war." The Senate noted, however, that this was a tentative judgment and the committee had been instructed to continue its deliberations. One of the comments of the committee had been a suggestion that Gumbel undergo a psychiatric examination because his behavior indicated a "demogogic [*sic*] nature."[13] There is no record of whether this was carried out. The Senate insisted that its reaction to Gumbel had no "political significance" since the judgment was unrelated to his "political beliefs." However, it added, a teacher of youth should not be involved in political activities.

The committee reported again on 11 March 1925, and this time there was a split vote. One opinion came from Baethgen and Dohna, and a separate one issued from Jaspers. In neither case was there a strong argument in his defense. Baethgen and Dohna thought that the reputation of the university should come before the individual; Jaspers focused on the fact that Gumbel had not been political in the classroom, and argued that his actions as a private citizen were not the responsibility of the university.[14]

---

[12]*HA*, 3, 5b, Nr. 333 (1924-1925).

[13]Carmon, "The University," 77.

[14]Jaspers' role in all of this merits special attention. He played an important part in the philosophical/psychological/educational debate about the need for wholeness or synthesis. See his *Die Idee der Universität* (Berlin: Springer, 1961) and *Die geistige Situation der Zeit* (Berlin: Walter de Gruyter and Co., 1947). The fact that his wife was Jewish no doubt helps to explain his lack of an anti-Semitic bias. It was later a cause of danger for him under the Third Reich, and in 1935 he was forbidden to teach. One senses that he truly believed in the need for academic freedom in the university; so although he may not have agreed with Gumbel in his pacifism or socialism, he defended him.

Meanwhile another incident had occurred that involved Gumbel.[15] On 19 January 1925 a peace group, *Friedensgesellschaft,* sponsored a lecture by Professor Hellmut von Gerlach of Berlin, a well-known pacifist. About six or seven hundred attended this lecture, including about one hundred or one hundred fifty students. As soon as the introduction was begun by Gumbel, some students started a fracas. The police appeared on the scene and quieted things down, apparently without violence. Nevertheless, the students complained to the rector—in a letter of 29 January—of the police's interference with their attempts to silence Gumbel. In subsequent weeks they renewed their demands for action by the university in the Gumbel case, which they claimed was important for the "entire German people."

On 16 May 1925 a final decision was reached by the Senate and published.[16] All but one of the philosophy faculty (presumably Jaspers) wished Gumbel to leave the university; yet in the name of academic freedom they would not insist upon it. They labeled him a "fanatical idealist" and a "pacifist," but since he was only a lecturer, they probably assumed that he would never be nominated to the regular faculty and so they let him stay. There is no suggestion that he was really entitled to have such divergent opinions, or that they would have been interested in discussing the substantive issues with him.

Soon after this decision by the Heidelberg professors, the scene shifted to Tübingen, where Gumbel was invited by a group of socialist workers and students to give a speech.[17] The rector of the university refused permission for the use of any lecture hall and warned the students not to sponsor Gumbel or even to take coresponsibility with the workers. His words of advice fell on deaf ears, however, and the students cosponsored the lecture and made arrangements to hold it at an inn in Tübingen—Hirsch's Inn. The later reports submitted by the Director of Police indicate complete surveillance of the meeting and serious disapproval of the students' activities. The topic for Gumbel's speech was "Political Murders" (the name of one of his earlier books), and the rector made clear his veto of such a topic; when it was suggested that Gumbel would change it to "Germany and France," he was no more amenable.

Those in charge of the lecture attempted to allow only those holding tickets to enter the room—presumably the socialist workers and students—but before long others attempted to gain entry and rioting broke out. The sponsors of the

---

[15]*HA,* 3, 5b, Nr. 431 (1925).

[16]*HA,* 3, 5b, Nr. 333 (1924-1925) "Beschluss der philosophiche Fakultät vom 16 Mai 1925 in der Angelegenheit des Privatdozenten Dr. Gumbel."

[17]*TA,* Nr. 2356, 4. Beil, 3 July 1925, and *TA,* Nr. 945, 3 July 1925. Reports from the rector to the Ministry and from the police inspector to the rector.

meeting then moved it to Lustnau, a suburb of Tübingen, but even there it became impossible for the speaker to address his audience.

Given the title of his talk, one can surmise that he spoke—or attempted to speak—about the discrepancy between the treatment of those who were responsible for murders of people on the Left—for example, of Rathenau, who had been assassinated in 1922—and of those who attempted to murder people on the Right. In an article published in 1928, Gumbel pointed out that from 1919 to 1922 there were 376 political deaths; 354 were from the Right and 22 from the Left. But only one from the Right—that of Rathenau—received any real recognition and "atonement."[18]

Another charge against Gumbel related to a letter that he supposedly wrote on 4 November 1924 to Frau Professor Quayzin in Murrhardt.[19] Quayzin was a teacher at the Katherinenstift in Stuttgart and wrote an article for a Swiss journal on the theme "Germany and the World War." In it she quoted Gumbel as agreeing in a letter to her that the Versailles treaty was unjust, but that it was not more so than the peace of 1871 or the peace between Germany, Russia, and Rumania at Brest Litovsk. Although Gumbel denied writing such a letter, the faculty at Heidelberg added it to the mounting evidence against him.

As to the reaction at the University of Tübingen, one is again faced with the unwillingness of colleagues to stand by Gumbel when he was accused of un-German statements. It was reported to the rector of Tübingen, Ludwig von Köhler, that Professor Robert Wilbrandt had been involved in extending the invitation to Gumbel to speak to the workers and students at Hirsch's Inn. Although von Köhler is referred to elsewhere as a "democrat," he was not sympathetic to Gumbel's ideas and he accused Wilbrandt of disloyalty to the university for providing an invitation to Gumbel. The rector told him that he found such conduct far more unacceptable in him than in the students. Wilbrandt, in reply, did not defend either Gumbel or his own freedom to explore socialist or pacifist thought; rather, he was "hurt" by the rector's rash judgment of him and denied having been party to Gumbel's invitation. Furthermore, he said that he had not been aware of Gumbel's opinions until he went to the lecture.[20]

---

[18]E. J. Gumbel, "Die Ursacher der politischen Morde," *Das Forum* 9:3 (December 1928). Walther Rathenau, foreign minister of the Republic, was a Jew and was murdered 24 June 1922.

[19]*HA*, 3, 5b, Nr. 433 (1925-1926).

[20]*TA*, 2356. Letter from von Köhler to Wilbrandt, 3 July 1925; Wilbrandt to Köhler, 4 July 1925. Robert Wilbrandt was a professor of national economy (1908-1929). See his *Ihr glücklichen Augen, Lebenserinnerungen* (Stuttgart: Franz Mittelbach, 1947).

This is rather difficult to believe since Gumbel had been speaking and writing since 1919, with six or seven books published before 1925. Deak, in his study of intellectuals in Weimar, claims that when Gumbel went to Heidelberg in 1923, "He was already well known and much hated for his pacifist politics and his shattering documentary revelations on patriotic murders and reactionary justice."[21] Although a mathematician, he was focusing on statistical studies of political murders.

When the whole Gumbel case was discussed in the *Landtag* of Württemberg on 11 July 1925, Wilbrandt asked the Minister of Culture and Education for a thorough investigation of the charge that he had been involved in the invitation to Gumbel. The request was denied.[22] It is clear that he did not use the opportunity to raise any questions about Gumbel's innocence—and yet, Wilbrandt was himself a Social Democrat. Theodore Eschenburg, in writing of Tübingen's atmosphere at the time when he began his own career there (1924), mentions Professor Robert Wilbrandt as one of the men whose personal friendship was generally shunned. He describes him as "a peaceful unassuming man," an unpolitical idealist who "pressed his Social Democratic convictions on no one but also never concealed them."[23] Why, then, did he so fear identification with Gumbel?

Meanwhile Gumbel continued his teaching, writing, and public speaking. Things seem to have quieted down at Heidelberg with the faculty decision not to deprive him of his *venia legendi*. However, when the question of promoting him to regular faculty status was raised by the Ministry, the reaction showed that nothing had really changed. In 1928 the Minister of Education and Culture took the initiative. He informed the faculty that he had received no complaints about Gumbel since 1925 and consequently he thought it was time to consider a promotion for him. He wished to know the opinion of the Senate regarding his regular lectures at the university. He was informed rather quickly that the faculty was opposed to his intention. And there the matter rested for another year. When Radbruch, Anschutz, and Lederer heard of this reaction on the part of the Senate, they filed a letter of protest with the rector and the Senate, testifying to their support for Gumbel.[24] There was no response.

---

[21]Istvan Deak, *Weimar Germany's Left-Wing Intellectuals* (Berkeley: University of California Press, 1968) 243.

[22]*WS*, Kulturministerium (Stuttgart), Nr. 1805, 20 April and 1 May 1926.

[23]Theodor Eschenburg, "Aus dem Universitätsleben vor 1933," *Deutsches Geistesteben und Nationalsozialismus—Eine Vortragsriche der Universität Tübingen* (Tübingen: University of Tübingen, 1965) 36. Professor Eschenburg amplified his remarks in an interview with the author, January 1972, in Tübingen.

[24]*HA*, 3, 5b, Nr. 332 (1930-1931) and Carmon, "The University," 80.

The following year the faculty nominated Dr. Hermann Glockner instead of Gumbel, but the Ministry did not act on the nomination. Instead, in July 1930 Dr. Adam Remmele, Minister of Education and Culture, approached the dean of the faculty with a compromise. If both Gumbel and Glockner were appointed to faculty status, would the professors accept it? The dean then discussed this possibility with two other members of the Small Senate, and they apparently agreed to the minister's proposal. Gumbel was then appointed to an associate professorship.[25]

During this time a subplot had developed around the proposed appointment of Gunther Dehn, a lecturer in theology at Magdeburg, to the Heidelberg faculty. His field of interest was the role of the church in questions of war, and he was personally a conscientious objector. Although the Minister of Education and Culture expressed approval for the appointment, the theology faculty rejected him and put pressure on the dean to withdraw the original faculty vote that had supported him. There was a clear division of opinion between the Small Senate and the Great Senate, the latter having a broader representation from the faculties than the former. Unfortunately, the debate centered on the procedures that had been followed by the Ministry rather than on any substantive arguments. Dehn decided to accept an appointment to Halle, and thus the questions remained unresolved.[26]

Its significance for the Gumbel case lay in the development of strong and vocal student opposition to such appointments. By November 1930 the National Socialist students had gained the upper hand in the AStA, even though they represented only twenty-one percent of the students. It was the affinity of their ideas with those of the other conservative students that gave them political power strong enough to manage the demonstrations against "un-German" faculty. They also succeeded in gaining allies from Heidelberg's civic groups, leaving the university officials at a loss to control them. The rector forbade "unsupervised political meetings" and the wearing of uniforms. In January 1931 the students staged a protest against Gumbel as "a Jew and un-German," claiming that they should not be subjected to such a teacher. At this point the police came on campus to quell the riot and the Ministry dissolved AStA.

The faculty denounced the police action and the Ministry's unilateral dissolution of the student council. Furthermore, they now insisted that the Ministry acknowledge publicly that it had made an error in promoting Gumbel.[27]

---

[25]Ibid.

[26]Carmon, "The University," 117-19.

[27]HA, 3, 5b, Nr. 332.

Throughout all these events a minority among the faculty—chiefly Rad-bruch, Anschutz, and Lederer—kept protesting the actions of the students and those who supported them. In an article in the *Heidelberger Tägeblatt*,[28] Pro-fessor Radbruch claimed that the students were going back to the Dreyfus case by confusing patriotism with anti-Semitism. On the other side of the debate, the leader seems to have been Willy Andreas, later elected rector (1932). He insisted that the State's appointment of Gumbel had been an interference with the rights of the faculty and warned the "liberals" that the same kind of inter-ference might sometime work against them. Andreas was a member of the DNVP and saw the instilling of the "feeling of nationalism" in the students as a faculty duty.

Such "nationalism" had, by 1931-1932, resulted in violent demonstrations by the students against Gumbel, whom they denounced as a pacifist and a Jew. In a letter to his friend Professor Radbruch, Albert Einstein commented on the action of the students as "one of the saddest signs of our times which honor so little the ideals of justice, tolerance, and truth."[29] To their credit we must note the counterprotests of Einstein, Karl Barth, Hajo Holborn, Emil Lederer, Gustav Radbruch, Ferdinand Tonnies, and Ernst Aster.[30] But they lost the battle; Gumbel was "released" from his teaching post on 5 August 1932.

Ringer points out that while the defenders of Gumbel had to take a public position on the case, the majority who were against him never had to come for-ward and explain their views. For him it is a classic example of the kinds of situations in which the "orthodox" could still "refuse to admit that their sup-posedly apolitical nationalism was quite as factional, divisive, and utilitarian in practice as the Social Democratic demand for reform."[31]

In the long run they and the National Socialists triumphed. In August of 1933 Gumbel was deprived of his citizenship and went into exile, first in Paris and then in the United States. He died in New York in 1966 after a full career as a prestigious mathematician at Columbia University.

When Gumbel was removed from his faculty post, only forty-two German professors were willing to sign a protest. The only one whom Gumbel men-tioned specifically was Anna Siemsen of Jena.[32] His colleagues at Heidelberg, for the most part, had shunned him since 1925. Professor Helmut Hatzfeld of

---

[28]Carmon, "The University," 86, quoting *Heidelberger Tägeblatt*, 11 December 1930.

[29]*HA*, 3, 5b, Nr. 332 (28 November 1930).

[30]Ringer, *The Decline*, 217.

[31]Ibid., 217-18.

[32]Emil J. Gumbel, ed., *Freie Wissenschaft* (Strasbourg: Sebastian Brant Verlag, 1938) 282.

The Catholic University of America recalled that as a new instructor himself at Heidelberg in 1932, he went to call on Gumbel as "one of the social amenities customary at a university," and was told that the professors were dismayed by his visit. He received a similar reaction when he visited Karl Jaspers, who had evidently suffered from his defense of Gumbel.[33]

All of the archival records dealing with the Gumbel case speak of his statements against war, his condemnation of a nationalistic approach to Versailles, and his refusal to honor German soldiers; no reports, except those of the student attacks, refer directly to the fact that he was a Jew. Was the climate at Heidelberg so anti-Semitic that it could be taken for granted? It is impossible to ascertain this, but in 1933 the American chargé in Stuttgart reported that Heidelberg would be only slightly affected by the Nazi laws respecting Jews and liberals because it had been known as nationalistic and anti-Semitic even before the takeover by the Nazis.[34]

On the other hand, one report from the *Landtag* in Stuttgart early in 1934 commented on the fact that Heidelberg had captured the field of economics because it had so many Jews on its faculty, being second only to Kiel.[35] This may, however, be illustrative of the charge that Ringer makes when he points out that in 1909-1910 there was a higher percentage of Jews in proportion to their numbers in society who were teaching at universities, but that only three percent of the full professors were Jewish and another four percent converts from Judaism. He maintains that there was little change in this picture from 1910 to 1930 and, in fact, anti-Semitism became more overt after World War I. Although the professors did not base their opposition to Jews on biological race, but rather on social and cultural differences, they nevertheless did see them as part of the whole Weimar culture of *Zersetzung* (dissolution).[36] If one goes by the numbers "purged" in Heidelberg after 1933, it would seem that Jews constituted about one-fourth of the teachers, presumably in the lower ranks of the faculties and among the *Dozenten*.

----

[33]Interview with Professor Hatzfeld, Washington, D.C., 12 April 1973. Interview with Herr Joseph Schwartz, Heidelberg, 16 January 1972. He had been a student at Heidelberg at the time.

[34]Chargé Dominian, Stuttgart, to U.S. Department of State, Washington, D.C., 1 May 1933, 862/42/61.

[35]A communication from Professor Oswald Lehnich, minister of economy for Württemberg, to the Staatsminister, 7 June 1934, *WS*, 763.

[36]Fritz Ringer, "The Perversion of Ideas in Weimar Universities," in Henry Friedlander and Sybil Milton, eds., *The Holocaust: Ideology, Bureaucracy, and Genocide* (Millwood NY: Kraus International Publications, 1980) 53-62.

The intolerance displayed toward Gumbel thus illuminates three elements that contributed to his downfall: pacifism, internationalism (or antinationalism), and the fact that he was Jewish. To what extent each of these was decisive is impossible to determine, but the combination of them was fatal. In much of the German nationalist criticism of Weimar these same elements are visible. Gumbel's colleagues at the university could not accept a new member into their ranks who so clearly identified with the Republic and whose understanding of the task of the university questioned so sharply their goal of *Kulturmission*. He was simply *persona non grata* and not even their dedication to academic freedom could shield him.

II

If Gumbel had been allowed to continue teaching at Heidelberg, he might have raised questions in his students' minds about the kind of nationalistic propaganda that was common rhetoric in the universities. His denunciation of war and his concern with "political murders" seriously confronted many of the opponents of the Weimar Republic and their attempts to keep alive the "war-guilt lie," the "stab-in-the-back" legend, and the idealization of *Langemarck*. With Nawiasky, the focus was on the Versailles treaty and the setting was the University of Munich.[37]

Hans Nawiasky had come to the university in 1918 and by 1928 had reached the rank of professor in the faculty of law, with a specialty in international law. He refused to give a nationalistic interpretation to the various questions that came within his field of competence, and for this he was attacked as early as 1922 by the National Socialists.[38] Although their own weakened condition after the abortive *Putsch* kept them from exerting significant influence on his career during the 1920s, the desire to block his rise in academia did not abate.

The first sign of real trouble came at a meeting of the *Akademischer Ortsgruppe des Vereins für Deutsches Ausland* on 25 February 1930. Nawiasky was selected, over the opposition of National Socialist students, as chairman to succeed the founder of the group, Professor Karl Rothenbucher. The National

---

[37]Hans Nawiasky, *Die Münchener Universitätskrawalle* (München, 1931). The basic story of the case, told here autobiographically, is substantiated in the protocols of the Senate at the University of Munich for these years. See "Senats-Niederschriften für die Studienjahre 1930-1932" in *MA*. As late as the spring of 1985, I have been unable to discover any personnel file at the university for Nawiasky; it apparently has been lost. No records were uncovered at the Bayerische Staatsarchiv in Munich that were relevant, except for some newspaper clippings.

[38]Ludwig Franz, "Der politische Kampf an den Münchener Hochschulen von 1929 bis 1933 im Spiegel der Presse" (dissertation, University of Munich, 1949) 105.

Socialist students evidently reacted with some violence, for at a meeting of the University Senate on 8 March, Professor Adolf Weber inquired whether any action had been taken by the university against the students who had so offended Professor Nawaisky. In response, the rector pointed out that the students were from the Technical Institute and not from the university itself; therefore, Professor Nawiasky could appeal to the Institute.[39] Nothing more is recorded in the minutes.

The sentiments of the NS students were echoed in the press. Like the students, those who attacked Nawiasky in the newspaper denounced his "Jewishness" and bemoaned the fact that such teachers were being given to German youth. Nawiasky had been born in 1880 in Graz, Austria, but his grandfather had lived in Czernowitz. It was later said that Nawiasky's origins in Eastern Europe might account for his "un-German" views. It was not uncommon for Germans to connect Jews with Eastern Europe; they were the stereotypical Jews found in much of German literature. The German Jew with a longer family history within Germany itself was seldom the target.[40] One senses that it was this kind of prejudice that was responsible for this early outburst against Nawiasky; the later conflict would deal with the content of his teaching.

The next step came in one of his classes in international law on 23 June 1931. The year in between had seen an attempt on the part of the university officials and the Ministry to discipline the National Socialist student organization (NSDStB) as it became more and more disruptive. For most of 1930 its members were not permitted to participate in university celebrations, and in the minutes of the Senate meetings there are several references to cases of student discipline that seem related to NS activities although the minutes do not give the complete details. Nevertheless, it is clear that in 1931 the students causing the trouble in Nawiasky's class were university students, not students at the Technical Institute.

What did Nawiasky teach that caused the outcry? He was dealing with the question of the rights and powers that one sovereign state can exercise over another. He pointed out that such rights can be acquired by peace treaties or can be imposed through conquest. Using such examples as railroad border checks made in Czechoslovakia, use of the harbor in Danzig by Poland, and the ninety-nine-year leases forced on China by the European powers in the nine-

---

[39]"Senats-Niederschriften," 8 March 1930, *MA*. The distinction between the Technical Institute and the University was, of course, a real one, but was there no communication between them?

[40]George Mosse, *Germans and Jews* (New York: Grosset and Dunlop, 1970) ch. 3, passim.

teenth century, Nawiasky explained how such "rights" may be written into general treaties—for example, Versailles. Even though such a treaty may be politically unwise or even unethical, it is "legal" and therefore the "rights" exist in law. He further pointed out that Versailles had followed the model of Brest-Litovsk and Bucharest (treaties made by Germany with Russia and Eastern Europe in 1917-1918) in that all three were treaties imposed on the conquered by the conqueror.[41]

That Nawiasky was aware of the general climate of opinion—which made anything other than outright condemnation of the Versailles *Diktat* unacceptable—was evidenced by his request that his remarks be kept within the classroom so that they would be understood within proper context. He did this, symbolically and with an attempt at wit, by saying to the students: "Be sure the windows are closed."

His suspicions were confirmed when the *Völkische Beobachter* of 26 June published an account of his lecture under the heading, "A Fine University Professor! Nawiasky Defends the Versailles Treaty." According to this article, Nawiasky had said, "Versailles, yes surely, *there* was done what we ourselves had done earlier in Brest-Litovsk and Bucharest." Interpreting this as a "French chauvinist" point of view, the authors of the article demanded that the university be cleared of such "un-German" elements as Nawiasky: "You have acknowledged the treaty of Versailles as justified; Versailles, which has perpetuated hate, mistrust, and discord in Europe; Versailles, which has burdened our German people with a dreadful fate; Versailles, which in all who still feel German burns as ignominy and disgrace." They further saw in his lecture a defense of the Weimar government's policy of fulfillment:

> You have acknowledged not only Versailles but also all that came after . . . the invasion of the Ruhr and the "Schlageter" deal, the Polish rape of the East, the ever-new humiliations in Spa, London, Genoa, Locarno, and Geneva . . . the subjugation brought about by Dawes and Young . . . the endless chain of German suffering, the misery and disgrace, the armies of unemployed, the confused, the suicides—all this you have acknowledged as justified.[42]

This attack in the National Socialist party organ makes it clear how the burgeoning organization played on the basic feelings of the German populace. If it could be demonstrated that a professor was "un-German," that is, that he held the Versailles treaty legally binding in international law and by inference supported the government's attempts to fulfill the terms of the treaty, then there

---

[41]Nawiasky, *Die Münchener*, passim.

[42]Ibid., 9.

would be sufficient grounds for demanding that he be removed from his teaching post. This, at least, seems to have been the assumption.

Nawiasky's defense, however, makes it impossible to judge whether or not the assumption was correct. He insisted that, taken out of context, his remarks suggested exactly the opposite of their real meaning; he had not upheld Versailles, merely compared it to Brest-Litovsk. "It says here [in the newspaper article quoted above] that I defended the Versailles treaty, while I have done exactly the reverse—sharply rejected it."[43] Moreover, in none of his remarks in the months that followed does one find any verbal defense of the Weimar government. It is known from other sources that he had worked on the constitutional reform in Bavaria and was close to Minister Held, the Bavarian minister of state. As a strong federalist, he may have had problems with the Weimar Constitution, but he certainly was regarded as a supporter of the democratic republic in general. After 1945 he was once again active in drawing up a new constitution for Bavaria.[44]

Yet the sole defense he offered in the long weeks of investigation (23 June-29 July 1931) was that academic freedom was being challenged. Nawiasky was of the opinion that if the content of his lecture was subjected to the scrutiny of even a friendly court, it would be a blow to what he regarded as the necessary academic freedom of the university. He knew, moreover, that his statements on international law would not be respected or supported by most of his colleagues. Even a remote comparison of Versailles and Brest-Litovsk set sparks flying. Dr. Lent, a professor of law at the University of Munich, delivered a preamble to the interpellation in the Bavarian court where Nawiasky's case was heard and probably represented the common view of the matter. He was of the opinion that Nawiasky had certainly not defended the Treaty of Versailles, but

> on the other hand it must be said that the remarks which he himself admits making were not only completely incorrect, but also must have given the impression that there was a weakening of German national feeling against Versailles. It will certainly have a weakening effect if one says that we ourselves have given a previous example for this heavy injustice. At this time I would like to say that this particular interpretation [that the treaties of Brest-Litovsk and Bucharest were the pattern for Versailles] was a view held in 1919-20 by political idiots in the Conference but in the last ten years no one has ever heard such nonsense, not even at political gatherings.[45]

---

[43]Ibid.

[44]Konrad Beyerle, *Zehn Jahre Reichsverfassung* (München: Max Huber, 1929) 32. Obituary for Nawiasky in *Universitätschronik* 1961/62.

[45]Nawiasky, *Die Münchener*, 22.

The case provided an opportunity for the academic community to defend itself against the intrusion of National Socialism. Nawiasky's emphasis on his academic freedom demonstrates that in 1931 it was clearly still possible to protest violations of this kind in civil court, a possibility that was soon to vanish. But it also demonstrates, sadly enough, that professors cared very little about their colleagues who were coming under fire from the radical students.

The Minister of Education and Culture for Bavaria, Dr. Goldenberger, spoke to the court about the nature of education and the importance of protecting it against undue State interference. More was at stake in the university than simply the communication of knowledge from teacher to student; the mission of both was to search for truth and to share ethical responsibility. The current trend, he argued, would lead to making knowledge the servant of the State, and this must be rejected at all costs. To deny academic freedom was to violate Article 142 of the Weimar Constitution.[46]

Nawiasky, speaking in his own defense, delivered a telling criticism of National Socialism. He insisted that it would produce a depersonalized man, "one who carries out central orders, a man who only serves, who has been torn away from his family. A sense of personal responsibility is contrary to blind obedience, to the 'adoration of *Führers*.' " He denounced both National Socialism and Communism as enemies of the real *Burgertum* (community of citizens). Further, he struck at the very heart of the German Nationalist position held by so many of his colleagues, calling "nationalism" unethical and egoistic when it is not based on respect for other nations as well as for one's own. Specifically, he denounced the National Socialist students for not respecting academic freedom, for already following blindly the decisions of a Führer, and for allowing themselves to sink into "mass man," putting the authority of the group above every other consideration. Nawiasky pointed out that such students were moving away from the middle-class values, among which he placed truth, honor, personal (but not blind) obedience, and awareness of belonging to a community, which makes strong adoration of a leader impossible. He insisted that an inherent contradiction existed between the Nazi party and the middle class, but most of all he found it incompatible with free decision making and, as such, out of harmony with true education.[47]

One would like to know more of what went on between Nawiasky and his colleagues at the university. His obituary in the *Universitätschronik* (1961-1962) makes no mention of the 1931 "incident." It does reveal that he was "released" from his teaching post in accordance with the law of April 1933 removing all

---

[46]Ibid., 26-29.

[47]Ibid., 35-38.

Jews from university posts. He spent the following years in St. Gallen, Switzerland, returning after 1945 to lecture again at Munich.[48]

The protocols of the Senate meetings of the university in the months of June and July 1931 indicate that the Nawiasky case was dealt with repeatedly and at length.[49] The defendant appeared at the meeting of 30 June, but the record simply states that he came, explained his position, and left. What he said and any discussions that ensued are not recorded.

What the protocols do reveal is that there were frequent disruptions of class by the National Socialist students and demonstrations sponsored by them in different parts of the university. The rector repeatedly warned them against such conduct, and finally the university was closed from July first to sixth. Extraordinary sessions of the Senate were held almost daily, but they seem to have dealt with the disciplinary issues more than with Nawiasky's teaching. The concern was with the proper procedures to be followed by the university officials, and there was constant communication between the rector and the Ministry to make sure that all was being handled properly.

A special committee of the faculty was appointed to study the charges against Professor Nawiasky. Unfortunately, the resolutions and other papers concerning Nawiasky referred to in this committee's report—and the report itself—are not available, possibly having been destroyed by university officials or lost in the destruction of the university library during the war. Some hope has been expressed that they will be rediscovered as the reorganization of the archives moves forward. It is noted in the protocols that on 25 July the rector reported to the Senate that the investigatory committee had examined all the relevant materials and would give a full report to Nawiasky, but it adds that the records of the committee would not be made available to him. The Senate approved of this action. Apparently, Nawiasky was not censured by his colleagues; neither was his name cleared.[50] Many questions remain unanswered. Did his colleagues agree with his evaluation of the National Socialist movement? If so, why didn't they make a public statement defending him? On the other hand, why didn't they censure him for his ideas, which were so contrary to their own?

According to Professor Kuhn at Munich, many of Nawiasky's other students defended him against the National Socialist students. The professors, in his view, refused to violate his academic freedom—a privileged tradition among

---

[48]*Universitätschronik* 1961/62.

[49]"Senats-Niederschriften" *MA*, passim.

[50]Ibid., 29 July 1931.

them.[51] Their "neutrality"—if one can call it that—said more about them than it did about him.

As in the case of Gumbel, the question of anti-Semitism inevitably arises. The only available records deal with procedures and charges concerning his teaching about Versailles; no mention is made of his race. Yet it is true that this was the reason given by the National Socialist press for rejecting him as chairman of the *Vereines für des Deutschtum in Ausland* in 1930. Undoubtedly his Jewishness was emphasized in the students' attacks. The professors would certainly not have stooped to such behavior in public, but what was their underlying prejudice?

Several authors—Bleuel, Faust, Ringer, and Bracher among others[52]— suggest that the 1920s witnessed increasing anti-Semitic thought and expression in academic circles. Ringer claims that "during the Weimar period, the long-established connections between mandarin anti-modernity and anti-Semitism became ever more overt."[53] Many professors identified Jewishness with Marxism, with Eastern European un-Germanness, and with the general disintegration of culture.

According to Bleuel, Lujo Brentano struggled against a spirit of anti-Semitism at the university in Munich and complained in 1924 that he could find very few colleagues to help him oppose it.[54] In 1925 at the national *Akademikertag*, a resolution was adopted urging that no more Jews be called to faculties.[55] In a letter to Arthur Hubscher of 27 June 1928, Thomas Mann recalled his own experience at the same university in the early 1920s. He spoke of the criticism leveled against him for being a "party person." Mann said that he had not become a party person, but "I do not hide the fact that I want to have nothing to do with people who said of Rathenau's assassination: 'Bravo, one less' (Munich University Professors!)."[56]

A subtle but pervasive anti-Semitism among the professors in Weimar is understandable, even if not acceptable, in light of their dedication to the

---

[51]Helmut Kuhn, ed., *Die deutsche Universität im Dritten Reich* (München: R. Piper and Co., 1966) 37.

[52]Bleuel, *Die Bekenner;* Ringer, *The Decline* and "The Perversion"; Karl Dietrich Bracher, *The German Dictatorship* (New York: Praeger, 1970); Faust, "Studenten and Nationalsozialistismus."

[53]Ringer, *The Decline*, 224.

[54]Bleuel, *Die Bekenner*, 123.

[55]Ibid., 189.

[56]Richard Winston and Clara Winston, eds. and trans., *Letters of Thomas Mann, 1889-1955* (Harmondsworth, England: Penguin Books Ltd., 1975) 148.

Kulturmission of the German nation, as they perceived it. The university's role was to assure the nation of future leaders imbued with the spirit of German "cultivation" (*Bildung*). Often enough, Weimar writers, artists, and dramatists were Jewish, and that fit with the professors' judgment that the new culture was "un-German."

Mosse has shown the complicated interrelatedness of Germans and Jews in the intellectual history of twentieth-century Germany. Perhaps the key to understanding the anti-Semitism of the professors is in his statement that the Jew was regarded as an outsider: "Culture was closed to him, for he lacked the necessary spiritual foundations."[57]

Given this perception of the Jew as outside of the German *Kulturmission*, how could the professors have been expected to defend their Jewish colleagues? Unfortunately most of them could not—or would not—rise above the general atmosphere of German anti-Semitism. Thus the professors became forerunners of the most virulent racism of modern times. If in the 1920s they could not admit that professors might legitimately deviate from the German Nationalist position on such things as the *Reich*, the *Völk*, the *Versailles Diktat*, or the war-guilt lie and still be entitled to a respectful hearing, could they later claim that the Nazis should refrain from imposing their *Weltanschauung* on the academic community as well as on all the other elements of society? By excluding dissenters from their midst, by failing to defend those who were different, the professors betrayed their own freedom and prepared the way for a totalitarianism that would overwhelm the university. The door was open to *Gleichschaltung*.

---

[57]Mosse, *Germans and Jews*, 60.

Chapter Five

1933: *Gleichschaltung*

As the door swung open on Hitler's Third Reich, it was evident that there was more continuity than discontinuity in German political life. The Nazis' rhetoric in 1933 is the key to understanding the success they had in subsuming all social institutions into the party. The language of German nationalism, already so much at home in academia, was inspiring and empowering. The goals of the government—honor to the Fatherland, restoration of Germanic lands to the Reich, revitalization of the German spirit—called forth loyalty and unity. The laws passed to effect that unity in 1933 met with little or no resistance from the university community.

Here again an English translation (coordination) is inadequate for the German *Gleichschaltung*. Helmut Krausnick suggests that the origin of the word is found in the electrical engineering term *Gleichrichter*, a rectifier that allows the passage of the electrical current in one direction only, thus changing alternating into direct current. The National Socialist party, in articulating its Leadership Principle, mandated a similar one-way movement of the Führer's will down to the people through every institution of society.[1] The power of the German people was henceforth to be channeled according to one norm only—the will of Adolf Hitler. Educational institutions, from kindergarten through university, were now given a role to play in this national revitalization.

From one point of view, the politicization of the German universities might be seen as starting in this moment; from another, it is the logical consequence of the German nationalist temper of the Weimar professors. The declining days of the Republic, with all their political vagaries and crises, were experienced by them as unpleasant but not unexpected. Never supporters of Weimar, the professors hoped that now there would be a restoration of "German" virtues

---

[1]Helmut Krausnick, "Stages of Co-ordination," in *The Road to Dictatorship, 1918-1933* (London: Oswald Wolff, 1964) 136.

of law and order, the appearance of a real leader who would represent the German nation and not a political party, and a resumption of the *Kulturmission* by the State.

Even the professors who had been designated as "Republicans of the Head" lost hope in the later years of Weimar. Alfred Weber and Friedrich Meinecke complained of the impotency of the Republic,[2] while Gustav Stresemann, foreign minister from 1925 to 1929, had to admit that he found himself hampered in all his efforts to direct foreign policy by the "constant strife which exists in the parliamentary system and the completely false attitude that parliament had toward its responsibility to the nation."[3] Disillusionment had taken its toll and, in a way, democracy had died in Germany in 1930 when Brüning had found it necessary to rule by presidential decree.[4]

Shifting voting patterns from 1930 to 1933 constituted adequate storm signals, but men continued to hope that the barometer was inaccurate when it recorded a great increase in the National Socialist representation. The SPD (Socialists) declined from 142 delegates elected to the Reichstag in September 1930 to 120 in March of 1933. The Democrats (DDP—where the "Republicans of the Head" tended to be counted) went from twenty to five while the People's party (DVP) declined from thirty to two. On the Right side of the ledger, the Nationalists (DNVP) increased from 41 to 52, and the National Socialists (NSDAP) went from 107 to 288. The Center held its own, even increasing from sixty-eight to seventy-four.[5] The hoped-for localization of power in sufficient strength to secure effective government was achieved, but at the cost of surrender to the extreme Right.

Reports from U.S. diplomatic personnel in Germany during these years (1930-1933) referred repeatedly to the growing discontent with the Republic and suggested that its days were numbered. The United States military attaché in Berlin, for example, made the observation in the summer of 1931 that there was a great desire for a dictatorship and Brüning might be appointed to that role. His own evaluation of the needs of Germany is revealing: "A dictatorship of this character, backed by the national prestige of its leaders and the support

---

[2] Kurt Sontheimer, *Antidemokratisches Denken in der Weimarer Republik* (München: Nymphemburger, 1962) 192, 213.

[3] Ibid., 194.

[4] The conservative desire for strong presidential power rather than parliamentary rule is well described in Karl Dietrich Bracher, *The German Dictatorship* (New York: Praeger, 1970) 171ff.

[5] Based on tables given in Koppel S. Pinson, *Modern Germany* (New York: The Macmillan Co., 1966) appendix B.

of the army, would, I believe, better suit the German temperament and German life than the brand of parliamentary government to which the nation has been subjected for the past twelve years."[6] The worldwide depression that began with the fateful crash of the New York Stock Market in August 1929 was only partly tempered by the Hoover moratorium on war debts and reparations declared in 1930. The fiscal stability experienced under the Weimar government since 1924 was at an end. The continued fear of those who would suggest Marxist communism as a solution to their economic ills pushed the middle and upper classes to the Right.

The eighty-year-old president, General von Hindenburg, accepted the strong drift to the Right and appointed Adolf Hitler as chancellor. He placed his confidence in the advice of Franz von Papen, who agreed to serve as vice-chancellor in a cabinet that had three National Socialists and nine others, all from the Right side of the political spectrum. Led by von Papen, these conservatives thought that they could exercise restraint within the government, fight off the inroads from the Left, and achieve their own nationalistic goals without surrendering to the Nazi ideology. Although there is some dispute about the extent to which big business supported Hitler, there is not much disagreement that it served as one more institution that was "coordinated" by the movement after March 1933.[7] The army, which had so often expressed disdain for the "Austrian corporal," agreed to accept his leadership and was eventually to take an oath of loyalty to him personally. The churches, formerly outspoken against the paganism of the Nazi program, reversed course and lifted the stringent rules forbidding membership in the party. Now that Hitler was the legitimate head of the government, he could no longer be opposed by the obedient citizen. By late March 1933 the Christian churches were ready to trust the word of the new chancellor when he proclaimed that the new German State regarded "both Christian confessions the most important factors for the maintenance of our folkdom."[8]

The movement claimed all along to be "above party," and to most Germans it had an enthusiasm and conviction of its own inner dynamism that was a refreshing change from Weimar. It spoke of their German values and it

---

[6]Colonel Edward Carpenter, U.S. military attaché in Berlin, to Department of State, 18 July 1931. Rpt. 11, 532; 2657-B-735.

[7]See, for example, the controversy stirred by David Abraham, *The Collapse of the Weimar Republic: Political Economy and Crisis* (Princeton: Princeton University Press, 1981) as described in the *New York Times*, 23 December 1984.

[8]Adolf Hitler, speech of 23 March 1933, *Völkischer Beobachter*, 24 March 1933. English translation is that given in Nuremberg Document No. 3387-PS.

promised a reintegration of all the forces in society around the goal of national prosperity and prestige.

The members of the university community did not stand outside the limitations of their own society; they, too, were hopeful in January of 1933. A few expressed doubt; some were perhaps more perceptive and more fearful of the new order. Despite the incidents of the past few years in which the Nazi students had shown themselves to be aggressive and disruptive, the professors believed that once a strong government was in power such incidents would cease. They, like many others, attributed the radicalism of the National Socialists to the party's strong anticommunist position and to its desire to recreate an image of a strong Germany vis-à-vis the Western nations. Once in power, so the argument ran, such techniques as street fighting and disruption of meetings and classes would not be necessary, and the leadership of the party would be able to control the young radicals. If this was what they thought, the professors certainly misunderstood and underestimated Herr Hitler.

The new chancellor, within the week of his appointment, had President von Hindenburg issue a decree entitled, "For the Protection of the German People." It was a euphemistic way of introducing censorship of newspapers and periodicals and mandating restrictions on all public gatherings.[9] The mysterious destruction of the Reichstag by fire on 27 February, even fifty years later a topic of historical investigation and speculation, was facilely attributed to the communists and furnished the pretext for a further stricture. By an ordinance of 28 February 1933 all basic rights guaranteed in the Weimar Constitution were suspended because of the "emergency." In time this would be known as the "Basic Law of the Third Reich," and it undergirded the entire totalitarian structure.

In the face of such repressive legislation, it may be surprising that the parties of the Right won an overwhelming victory in the elections of 5 March 1935. But it is not surprising if one acknowledges the widespread fear of communism and accepts the indictment of the communists in the burning of the Reichstag as the reason for the emergency decree, and also not surprising if one can envision the SA presence, which guarded against vocal dissent.

Now that Hitler was the "legal authority" in the State, those who did oppose him went underground. Civil resistance to law had never been developed within the German legal tradition[10] and so in these early years one finds little overt opposition to the new regime.

---

[9]Krausnick, "Stages," 138.

[10]Mary Alice Gallin, *The German Resistance to Hitler: Ethical and Religious Factors* (Washington: The Catholic University of America Press, 1955) ch. 3. The lack of a tradition of civil disobedience in German philosophical and theological thought made it very difficult for those who opposed Hitler to find proper grounding for their position.

By a vote of 444 to 94 the Reichstag on 23 March passed the "Enabling Act," by which legislative power was transferred from itself to the Cabinet; only the Social Democrats remained opposed. Although the Weimar Constitution was not publicly repudiated, its very fiber had disintegrated. In 1934 the transition to the empire known as the "Third Reich" would be accomplished, and the path to absolute dictatorship would be traversed inexorably.

Within a few months after the Enabling Act had been passed, laws were passed "coordinating" trade unions, student associations, the *Lände*, the political parties, and the churches. By 6 July 1933 Hitler could declare: "The Party has now become the State."[11] The electric current from here on would indeed travel in one direction only. The political parties, with the exception of the SPD, had dissolved themselves, and the SPD was banned by the government. The German Christian Church had come into line, even though some dissidents now formed the German Confessing Church. The Roman Catholic bishops were working with the Vatican for a concordat with Hitler that would guarantee the rights of the church—a move that would, however, also give "recognition" to the Hitler government by an international power. The "uncoordinated" factions were the pacifists, socialists, communists, small independent church groups, and some individual Jews and Christians. As "un-German" elements in society, they remained outside of the *Gleichschaltung*.

For the universities, what did "coordination" mean? The first direct blow was the law of 7 April 1933 entitled "Reorganization of the Career Public Service." Traditional academic freedom had provided for the selection of new faculty members through a process of nomination by the professors and ratification and appointment by the Minister of Culture and Education. Deans and rectors were chosen by the faculties, and the State complied with the formality of recognizing them. With the passage of this new law, two major changes were made: 1) certain persons would be henceforth excluded a priori from university teaching and could not be nominated; and 2) the Leadership Principle of National Socialism would substantially alter the role of the rector.

The law called for the immediate dismissal of all those who were "non-Aryan" and defined that designation in terms of those who had at least one parent or grandparent who was non-Aryan. Future marriages with non-Aryans would also be cause for exclusion from the faculties. Sensitive, however, to the admiration of war heroes that was noticeable among the professors and in deference, no doubt, to President Hindenburg, the Hitler government exempted certain persons from the law:

---

[11]Krausnick, "Stages," 149.

1. Those employed continuously by the university
   since 1 August 1914.
2. Those who fought in the Great War.
3. Those who had a father or son killed in the war.

The wartime record of a man was seen as possibly redemptive, but his racial origins became a heinous crime.

On the part of the university community there is no record of a call to defend academic freedom in the face of such discriminatory legislation. There is only a silence that is understandable but, with hindsight, certainly regrettable.

On 13 April sixteen professors were given a "leave of absence" from the universities in Prussia. Included in this number were: Marck, Kelsen, Lederer, Bonn, Heimann, Tillich, Mannheim, Lowe, Sinzheimer, and Herkheimer.[12] By the first of May, the United States consul in Stuttgart was reporting that the situation for "liberal minded university professors" had become intolerable, and Jews had been compelled to resign in Berlin, Heidelberg, Tübingen, Göttingen, and Frankfort. He commented further that the entire faculty of medicine at the University of Berlin had been depleted.[13]

The purging of the Jewish faculty members was followed on 26 April 1933 with a law setting quotas for Jewish students. The admission of Jewish students was to be henceforth limited to 1.5 percent of the incoming class.[14] All of the student clubs and fraternities that were primarily Jewish were under close surveillance and in the following months were outlawed. Communist, Socialist, and pacifist student organizations were also forced to cease operations and the *Deutsche Studentenschaft*, in most cases, sided with the Nazis in implementing the new regulations.[15]

The law of 26 April was entitled "Law to Prevent Overcrowding of German Schools and Universities," but it was clear that its real purpose was anti-Semitic.[16] In addition, it revealed the way in which the government understood

---

[12]Emil Gumbel, ed., *Freie Wissenschaft* (Strasbourg: Sebastian Brant, 1938) 273.

[13]Report from U.S. Consul Dominian in Stuttgart to Department of State, 1 May 1933, #876.42/6.

[14]Michael Stephen Steinberg, *Sabers and Brown Shirts* (Chicago: University of Chicago Press, 1977) 134.

[15]Ibid., 135-36.

[16]It was quite obvious to those who were on the scene. See the report of George Gordon, U.S. chargé in Berlin, to the Department of State, 2 May 1933, #862.42/59. A very thorough reflection on the events of 1933 is contained in a lengthy report from the U.S. consul in Leipzig, Ralph Busser, to the Department of State, 3 January 1934, #862.4212/19. This report received special commendation from Ambassador Dodd in his report to the Department of State, 26 January 1934, #862.42/20.

the purpose and mission of the university. The law's stated purpose was to reduce the number of graduates seeking employment in professional and industrial fields and to create a situation in which only those students who had "intellectual and physical maturity," "moral character," and "political reliability" would be educated. The secondary schools were to continue the task of identifying potential university students, but the state officials would actually select them.[17] "Political reliability" would rather rapidly come to mean service in the Hitler Youth and conformity to the dogma of National Socialism. Such a rephrasing of the *Kulturmission* of the German university was quickly adopted by those who wished to carry out the "national purpose." Staatsminister Bebemeyer, in addressing the university community at Tübingen in July of 1933, articulated the duties of students in this order: 1) training in labor for the State; 2) development of body and mind for the defense of the State; and 3) study.[18] For a man who had previously been on the faculty of the university, it was certainly a strange philosophy of education.

In keeping with the disdain previously expressed by most of the professors for ordinary "politics," they acted in 1933 as if these new laws and the implementation of them were no concern of theirs. When James Frank, a Jewish Nobel Peace Prize winner, resigned his chair at the University of Göttingen in protest against the law that "released" so many of his colleagues, thirty-three faculty members condemned his action as "sabotage" against the new government. They further expressed the hope that "the government will speed up the requisite cleansing measures."[19]

One of the greatest blows to the integrity of the academic community fell when Martin Heidegger accepted the rectorship of the University of Freiburg from the hands of the new regime. Many have found his position inexplicable in the face of the dismissal of his former teacher, Edmund Husserl, from his teaching post because of his Jewish background. Heidegger seemed to deny his own philosophical position when he stated in his inaugural address: "Not theses and ideas are the laws of your being! The *Führer* himself, and he alone, is Germany's reality and law today and in the future."[20] By the end of a year,

---

[17]Regarding the implementation of this law, see Report of Henry Leverich, vice-consul in Berlin, to the Department of State, 8 March 1935, #862.42/99.

[18]Report of Paul Gray, vice-consul, Stuttgart, 14 July 1933, to the Department of State, #862.42/67.

[19]Richard Grunberger, *The 12-Year Reich* (New York: Rinehart and Winston, 1971) 308, quoting *Frankfürter Zeitung*, 28 April 1933.

[20]Bracher, *German Dictatorship*, 268, quoting Martin Heidegger, *Die Selbstbehauptung der deutschen Universitäten* (Breslau, 1934) 22ff.

he was disillusioned, realized his dreadful mistake, and took the road to self-imposed exile in the Black Forest.[21] Heidegger was one of the better-known professors to have acted in this way, but he was from all reports not atypical.

The speech of the pro-rector, Professor Otto Heinrich Ermannsdorffer, at the University of Heidelberg to welcome the return of the black-red-white flag and its place alongside the swastika has already been noted.[22] At Tübingen the chancellor, Dr. August Hegler, resigned and it was simply announced that at this time no one would be named to the post.[23] The chancellor had been the liaison person between the university and the ministry—in many instances the position was purely honorary—but now that the State would be appointing the rector, it was considered unnecessary. On 24 April 1933 the State of Württemberg appointed a new official called a "commissar" who would be accountable to the Minister of Culture and Education, and the person chosen for this was Professor Bebemeyer. His speech, noted above, revealed a high degree of affinity with the Nazi rhetoric. In addition to making their goals for university education his own, Bebemeyer said that he sought a *Völkische* political and economic community of workers that would work toward a "breakthrough of the German soul." Did he realize that his betrayal of the university would lead, by 1938, to the incongruity of a rector appearing for his inauguration at Tübingen with the insignia of his office over his SA uniform?[24]

No doubt many professors were deluded by the language of the new government with its emphasis on the need to reaffirm Germany's national strength and honor, a goal in complete harmony with the traditional mandarin concerns for German *Kultur* and *Kulturmission*. Bracher has summed up the essential elements in the Nazi program that, in his opinion, appealed to the professors:

1. A new, essentially imperialistic nationalism.
2. A conservative and authoritarian glorification
    of an all-powerful State.

---

[21]Helmut Kuhn, professor of philosophy at Munich, expressed the opinion that Heidegger never really recovered from this brief affiliation with the Nazis in terms of his personal integrity and professional standing. He died in 1976. Interview with the author, 9 October 1971, Munich.

[22]See above, 41.

[23]It would be a mistake to read much into Hegler's act of resignation. It was probably an act of compliance with the Nazi government rather than an act of resistance. See *TU* protocols, 24 April 1933 and *WS*, Kultusministerium No. 762.

[24]In 1964 the student newspaper at Tübingen reprinted a photograph of this unusual garb. Tübingen, *Notizen*, February 1964.

3. A nationalistic-statist aberration of socialism, seeking
to combine social romanticism and state socialism.
4. A *völkisch* community ideology based on race.[25]

Although the professors and students varied considerably in their adherence
to the "racial" myth, they were at one in emphasizing the community aspects
of the *Völk* and thus became easy prey for those who were convinced that the
greatest obstacle to a strong *völkisch* nation was the presence of "un-German"
elements within it. The other points in the Nazi platform were all consonant
with the long-standing desires of the German National Conservatives, with
whom the professors were ideological soul mates even when they were not active members of the DNVP.

Among those who capitulated to the Nazi pressure were, in addition to
Heidegger and Bebemeyer, Willy Andreas, Hans Freyer, Erich Jaensch, Felix
Druger, Phillip Lenard, Karl Alexander von Müller, Julius Petersen, Wilhelm Pinder, Erich Rothacker, Carl Schmitt, Werner Sombart, Othmar Spann,
Johannes Stark, and Theodor Vahlen.[26] The degree of delusion varied, and the
speed with which disillusionment followed was also not uniform. Nevertheless, it is true to say that as a group they succumbed to the "system" because
of the acceptability of the ideals expressed by the Nazis. The rhetoric had a
familiar ring in the halls of academia.

What was new, however, was the method used to achieve these goals. The
National Socialist regime assumed not only control over faculty appointments
but also over curricula. Since all education, according to the party, was to have
a special role in the development of German history and culture, courses in
racial biology, geo-politics, folk music, Aryan physics, and other "relevant"
fields were made mandatory. Philosophical and theological faculties were
sharply reduced, and the work of historians was carefully monitored to see that
what they wrote supported Nazi claims. The oft-proclaimed dedication to
"pure" *Wissenschaft* was replaced by the State's determination of what was true
and useful in all fields of learning. As one minister of culture told the professors: "From now on, it will not be your job to determine whether something
is true, but whether it is in the spirit of the National Socialist revolution."[27]
Unfortunately, there are also examples of professors who spoke in the same
way, thereby confirming Hitler in his disdain for scholars. One such comment

---

[25]Bracher, *German Dictatorship*, 10.

[26]Fritz K. Ringer, *The Decline of the German Mandarins* (Cambridge MA: Harvard
University Press, 1969) 442. See also Bracher, *German Dictatorship*, 266-67.

[27]Bracher, *German Dictatorship*, 268, citing an address by Minister of Culture Hans
Schemm at the University of Munich, 1933.

was that of the Göttingen historian Ulrich Kahrstedt in 1934: "We renounce research for the sake of research. Sieg Heil!"[28]

Those professors who would not lend themselves to this cultural prostitution were quickly "retired." Brief notices appeared in local newspapers as the professors disappeared. Most of them followed the path of "inner migration," which meant retirement to their study to pursue scholarly concerns "in serenity" until the nightmare should be over.[29]

In addition to imposing academic controls on the professors and what they taught, the National Socialist government required "political activity" of all teachers, including those in higher education. Attendance at communal camps and instructors' academies became prerequisites for appointments and promotions. The junior faculty, anxious to please the new authorities, was generally more ready to embark on these experiences. Never having been admitted to the decision-making process in the Weimar universities, they were often swayed by promises of professional advancement and increased economic benefits. The party exerted control over the universities through the rectors they appointed and also through the leaders of the teachers' league and the student organizations.[30]

The German "Mandarins," to revert to Ringer's descriptive phrase once more, lost control of their own citadels. In the first year after the Nazi seizure of power, more than 1,600 scholars were retired or sent into exile.[31] Hartshorne claims that the number of outright dismissals of teaching faculty between 1933 and 1937 was 1,145.[32] Another author claims that fourteen percent of those teaching in the universities were removed or resigned between 1933 and 1945.[33] One of the difficulties in citing statistics here, as elsewhere, is that

---

[28]Ibid., 272.

[29]It was Gerhard Ritter who described the faculty at Freiburg in these terms of "serene scholar." "German Professors in the Third Reich," *Review of Politics* 8 (April 1946): 242-54.

[30]The significant changes in the concept of university rector that came with Nazism are evaluated in Helmut Seier, "Der Rektor als Führer," *Vierteljahrshefte für Zeitgeschichte* 12 (1946): 104-46. A complete description of the effect that this change had on the universities was sent by U.S. Ambassador Dodd to the Department of State, 10 December 1936, #862.42/132. See also directives of Bavarian *Kultusminister* in Haushofer file, Institut für Zeitgeschichte, Munich, #MA 619S.737.

[31]Bracher, *German Dictatorship*, 269.

[32]Edward Yarnall Hartshorne, *The German Universities and National Socialism* (Cambridge MA: Harvard University Press, 1937) 93.

[33]Christian von Feber, *Die Entwicklung des Lehrkorpers der deutschen Universitäten und Hochschulen, 1864-1954* (Göttingen: Vandenhoeck and Ruprecht, 1956) 143-46 for a statistical analysis of German emigrants.

some authors include both universities and technical institutes and others do not. There is also the problem of separating those who were expelled as "non-Aryan" and those who retired or were retired because they refused to collaborate with the regime. The overall picture, nevertheless, represents a disastrous loss to the German academic community. Noticeable gaps were created in all faculties; those of medicine and law were hardest hit. Men in the humanities and social sciences were numerous among the victims, and the demise of German scholarship was a foregone conclusion of the Nazi policy. As time went on, the list became ever longer: Ernst von Aster, Karl Barth, Ernst Cassirer, Wolfgang Koehler, Hans Rothfels, Otto Meyerhof, Albert Einstein, Fritz Haber, Moritz Julius Bonn, Jonas Cohn, Richard Honigswald, Werner Jaeger, Emil Lederer, Kurt Lewin, Robert Liefmann, Karl Mannheim, Franz Oppenheimer, Joseph Schumpeter, and Max Wertheimer.[34] The plaque in the entrance hall at the New School of Social Research in New York City is abundant testimony to the intellectual richness that made a path across the Atlantic during the Hitler era; indeed, many of the names cited above are on it.

The question that surfaces in such a reflection on the number of German émigrés is, "What did their colleagues at the universities do about it?" Many of the professors had long expressed disdain for the rowdy NS students, and now they felt the same about the "brown professors" who sold out to the party. But did they express anger at the shameful interference of the State in the affairs of the university? Did they protest the expulsion of so many scholars from their midst? The argument from silence is strong. By not defending their colleagues and the integrity of the disciplines they taught, they lost the war in the very first battle. The year 1933 was crucial, and it slipped through the fingers of those very persons who were famous throughout the world for their careful research and their critical thinking. There was apparently no transfer of these values to the political scene—what were the facts? and how were programs to be measured?—and the professors' inability to take a united stand in the face of the attack on the universities gave the Nazis the opportunity of knocking them off one by one.

The instance of James Franck's resignation at Göttingen was cited above; who was willing to stand with him? On 1 May 1933[35] the United States chargé in Berlin reported a similar case. Professor Eduard Spranger had resigned his

---

[34]Ringer, *The Decline*, 440-41.

[35]Chargé Gordon, Berlin, to the Department of State, 1 May 1933, #862.42/60. For Spranger's own account, see Eduard Spranger, "Mein Konflikt mit der national-socialistichen Regierung 1933," in *Universitas: Zeitschrift für Wissenschaft, Kunst, und Literatur* 10 (1955): 457-74.

chair at the University of Berlin in protest against the inaction of the rector and the minister of education toward the students who had posted anti-Semitic notices on the bulletin boards. Although Spranger had previously defended the National Socialist students when Rector Theodor Litt wanted to impose restrictions on them, he was now indignant at their attacks on Jewish writers. In a list of denunciations they posted, the students insisted that Jews must be prohibited from publishing works in the German language unless they indicated that they were "translations." The rationale behind this was that for a Jew to write in German was a "lie." Jewish words must be published in Hebrew; otherwise, the public will be misled. Spranger said that he was worried because the student organizations "were beginning to assume an attitude which reminded one strangely of Metternich's attitude toward professors and students." Evidently his earlier view that "the national movement among the students was still genuine at the core, only undisciplined in its form" was undergoing revision. And he had the courage to condemn the Prussian Ministry for not disciplining the students. Nevertheless, his resignation was accomplished in solitude.

Berlin was clearly ready for the book burning that occurred on 10 May 1933. Dr. Goebbels, minister of propaganda in the new regime, presided over the ceremony in which more than 20,000 books were destroyed. The authors on the blacklist included: Arthur Schnitzler, Alfred Doeblin, Leon Feuchtwanger, Emil Ludwig, Erich Maria Remarque, Thomas Mann, Jacob Wassermann, Upton Sinclair, Jack London, Ernest Hemingway, and Count Richard Coudenhove-Kalergi.[36] True, the Berlin University professors did not take part in the book burning and were scolded by the Prussian minister of education for "failing to lead their students in their fight for a new state,"[37] but what did they do to dissuade them?

The data are spotty but suggestive of painful times within the universities. When a person resigned for reasons of conscience, as in the case of Fritz Lieb at Bonn, a statement was often made. Emil Gumbel records Lieb's farewell to the theological faculty in November of 1933:

> I came here in order to say what was right and wrong as a evangelical theologian, preaching the Word of God in freedom and in obedience to that particular task. I felt myself—although I am and will remain a Socialist—never bound by that role to the line of a particular political party. I saw myself happily serving the German people. The possibility of this kind of teaching has now been taken from me by force. And because only the Word of God can bind a theologian, I am making herewith an explicit protest. God's Word in the Gospel has already

---

[36]Chargé Gordon, Berlin, to the Department of State, 12 May 1933, #862.428/8.
[37]Ibid.

been spoken to you and while I can do no more as a teacher I shall stand as a simple Christian working for the same end. I would like to ask you, unconcerned about the other expressions of this single Word, to remain true and obedient to it. With this request I take leave of you.[38]

A colleague of Spranger at Berlin, the well-known psychologist Wolfgang Koehler, director of the Institute of Psychology at the university, was also forced to leave his post. He had been one of the participants in the Weimar meeting called by Meinecke in 1926. A leader in the development of Gestalt psychology, Koehler was perhaps too well known a public figure to be openly attacked by the Nazis despite his criticisms of the party. Carroll Pratt has written of him:

> Friends of Koehler admired his courage (in refusing to accept the interference of the Nazis), though at the same time they were apprehensive lest in some mysterious way he might one day be removed from the scene. But nothing happened. And also nothing of importance happened within the University where Koehler had hoped he might arouse his colleagues to take some sort of action. In his efforts he met only frustration. Most of the professors either dismissed the Nazis as a bunch of thugs who could never gain control of the political machinery of the most advanced society of the world or refused as scholars to become involved in matters that were none of their business or outside their proper spheres or influence.[39]

Helmut Kuhn identified Koehler as a "passionate anti-Nazi." He recalls visiting with him in Berlin soon after he had published an outspoken criticism of the regime and finding him beating wasps in the garden. He laughingly explained his action by saying that, like the SA, they were "fat and brown." In 1934 the dismissal came, and Koehler left Berlin to begin a new and fruitful career at Swarthmore College in Pennsylvania.[40]

It is possible that there was some behind-the-scenes activity among the professors in support of their ousted colleagues, but there is little evidence of it. One example of brotherly concern is found in the account given by Max Planck of a visit he had with Hitler early in 1933.[41] Planck was at that time the president of the Kaiser Wilhelm Gessellschaft and had the task of making a report to the chancellor. He thought it a good opportunity to speak on behalf of his Jewish colleague, Fritz Haber. Hitler insisted, in response, that he had nothing against the Jews; it was just that they were all communists and therefore

---

[38]Gumbel, *Freie Wissenschaft*, 271.

[39]Wolfgang Koehler, *The Task of Gestalt Psychology*, intro. Carroll Pratt (Princeton: Princeton University Press, 1969).

[40]Helmut Kuhn, interview, 9 October 1971.

[41]*Die Erlanger Universität*, 15 November 1947, 1:22:336-37, quoting *Physikalische Blätter*, Heft 5, 1947.

his enemies. To Planck's remonstrance that one must distinguish among Jews because some of them came from old German families and were highly cultivated, Hitler answered: "That is not correct. A Jew is a Jew; all Jews stick together like burrs. Wherever there is one Jew, other Jews will gather. It was the task of the Jews themselves to show the distinctions among them and they have not done so; therefore, I must go against all Jews with equal strength." Planck pleaded further, invoking the economic importance of the Jews and the great loss to the country if they were to emigrate, but Hitler would not be moved. Planck left in despair.

The hopelessness of protest increased in the years from 1933 to 1936. The establishment of the central Ministry of Education in Berlin, with authority over the entire educational system in Germany, made nonconformity a basis for charges of "treason." Increasingly, professors chose the road to exile or the one of "inner migration." By 1936 the U.S. ambassador, William Dodd, could report: "The universities have thus been deprived of the place they once held as centers of German intellectual life."[42] According to him, by that time all the disciplines within the university had suffered because nothing could be taught that conflicted with "Nazi faith."

There were some instances, naturally, of men who would not bow to this Nazi dictum. Kurt Huber, who later joined the resistance group around the Scholls and other students at the University of Munich, refused to forge connections that the party wanted between music and German folklore.[43] Friedrich Meinecke was forced to resign as editor of the *Historische Zeitschrift* in 1936 because he would not "adjust" the articles to conform to racist ideology.[44] Gerhard Ritter claimed that he himself survived only because there were ways of circumventing the regime. His publications during the Nazi years, *Frederick*

---

[42]Dodd to the Department of State, 10 December 1936, #862.42/132.

[43]Huber was born in Switzerland of German parents in 1893, received his doctorate in Munich in 1917, and taught there in the fields of music, philosophy, and psychology until 1937 when he was called to Berlin. Here he was placed at the National Archives of Folk Songs, but his stay was short-lived because of his refusal to bend his disciplines to Nazi ideology. Despite this, he apparently joined the NSDAP in 1940, but later became a member of the Scholl group. He was hanged with them in February 1943. There is no complete dossier on him at the University of Munich, to which he had evidently returned from Berlin. There is only a brief collection of essays by some of his friends published as Clara Huber, ed., *Kurt Huber zum Gedachtnis* (Regensburg: Josef Habbel, 1947).

[44]Friedrich Meinecke (1862-1954) was long the dean of German historians. His attitude toward the Nazi State is well described in Robert Pois, "Friedrich Meinecke and German Politics in the Twentieth Century" (dissertation, University of Wisconsin, 1965). See also the excellent bibliography by Anne-Marie Reinold in *Historische Zeitschrift* 174 (1952): 503-23.

the Great (1936) and *On the Power State* (1940) were disguised attacks on the Third Reich that, according to him, were understood as such by his colleagues, but not by the less-intelligent ministers of the government.[45]

Ritter also felt that, despite the controls of the totalitarian state, one did well to continue the work of education. He found teaching during these years the best way of communicating values: "The mission of the modern historian was a thankful and beautiful one in the Third Reich."[46] He appreciated the opportunity to counteract the ideology that he found so distasteful and thus remained at his post in Freiburg. Later, he wrote: "How clearly did I then see that the mission of the university teacher was to give clear vision, a sure footing, sound principles and to transmit great traditions to an unbelieving, mistrustful and perplexed generation of youth."[47] Between 1938 and 1942 this "serene scholar" (a phrase used by Ritter to describe the goal of his colleagues at Freiburg) found it increasingly difficult to get permission from the government to accept invitations to lecture abroad. In November 1944 he was arrested by the Gestapo for incrimination in the July 1944 plot to assassinate Hitler. The basis for the charge was that he had been a friend of Carl Goerdeler and a member of the Confessing Church.[48] Ritter, however, survived the final days of the Reich and was one of the few persons close to the scene who was able to reflect on the life of the university community during those years. His own views remained "nationalist" and "conservative" until the end.

The use of parallel situations—a device in Ritter's historical writings—was also used by Hermann Oncken in his biography of Robespierre, *The Incorruptible*. It was a scathing attack on the dictatorship of the French Revolutionary hero, but it was also intended as a challenge to the Hitler regime.[49] Oncken, it will be remembered, was the speaker on many of the occasions when the Foundation of the Reich was celebrated at the University of Munich in the late 1920s. His speeches were thoroughly imbued with the spirit of the German

---

[45]Ritter, "German Professors," 245-46.

[46]Ibid., 248.

[47]Ibid.

[48]Ibid. See also some mention of Ritter's relationship to the resistance movement in Peter Hoffman, *The History of the German Resistance, 1933-1945* (Cambridge MA: MIT Press, 1977) 184, and his own *Carl Goerdeler und die deutsche Widerstands bewegung* (Stuttgart: Verlags-Anstalt, 1956).

[49]This, at least, seems to be the generally accepted understanding of Oncken's intention. This "use" of history—by both Ritter and Oncken—raises interesting questions for the professional historian. Does not such "slanting" of history to achieve a contemporary goal militate against its value as history of a particular era?

Kulturmission and supportive of an aggressive nationalistic foreign policy. After Munich, he was awarded a chair at the University of Berlin in 1928, and as a prominent lecturer there he attracted many students both from Germany and abroad. One of these, Professor Felix Hirsch of Trenton State College, refers explicitly to a lecture given by Oncken in 1933 (after Hitler's accession to power) in which he attacked Oliver Cromwell in such a way that he made his position toward the new government quite clear.[50]

His opposition to National Socialism led to a complaint against him by Walter Frank, minister of the Reich Historical Institute, in 1935. Oncken was now seen as "too liberal" and as subversive of the regime because he influenced his students to demonstrate on his behalf against a personal attack leveled against him in the *Völkischer Beobachter*.[51] Because of this, Frank proceeded to bring about an "early retirement" for Oncken, working through a colleague more sympathetic to National Socialism, Karl Alexander von Müller, to find a more cooperative person for the chair at Berlin. Von Müller also informed the Reich minister of education that Oncken was planning a dinner party on 22 March 1935 for the members of the Reich Historical Commission, "thereby winning a vote of confidence for himself [Oncken] personally and support for opposition to the State and the Movement."[52]

Another colleague of Oncken in his days at Munich, Karl Vossler, represents a more direct brand of opposition. As rector in 1927 he had shown support for the Weimar Republic by raising the black-red-gold flag on the occasion of the Jubilee of the university and had also urged students to open the doors of their corporations to their Jewish brethren.[53] When the Nazis took over in 1933, they lost little time in awarding him an "emeritus" rank, thus easing him out of his teaching career. But in the early days of the regime, the leaders wanted to indicate to the scholars abroad that German professors had lost nothing of their freedom to pursue learning and thus encouraged men like Vossler to accept speaking engagements when offered by foreign scholars. The text of their remarks on such occasions was, however, subject to prior review, and Vossler

---

[50]Letter from Professor Felix Hirsch, Trenton State College, in *Frankfürter Allgemeine Zeitung*, 26 August 1966.

[51]Institut für Zeitgeschichte, Munich, files MA 164 S. 13-18. The work of the Reich Historical Institute is well covered in Helmut Heiber, *Walter Frank und sein Reichsinstitute für Geschichte des neuen Deutschlands* (Stuttgart: Deutsches Verlags Anstalt, 1966).

[52]Ibid., file 596 S. 299-300; see the references to von Müller's work above, 32.

[53]See above, 40, 41.

became aware that his movements when he was out of the country were carefully monitored.

Finally, in 1941 he decided to accept no more invitations since he believed they spelled complicity in the Nazi propaganda. In a courageous letter written to the authorities, he told them he was being used as a "front" for the regime and did not wish to cooperate in their deceit.[54] He chose, rather, to live quietly in a suburb of Munich, doing advanced philological studies until the war was over. The Occupation forces appointed him rector of Munich once again in 1946.

To what extent can such noncooperation be termed "resistance"? In 1947 at a university ceremony honoring a group of students, the so-called Scholl group or "White Rose" cell who were executed by the Nazis in 1943, Rector Vossler expressed repentance for the academic community's insensitivity at that time to the students' fate: "Neither the Rector nor the Senate nor the Student organization took the risk of asking clemency for these pure children of academia."[55] Did he regret his own "inner migration," which had removed him from the university at that moment? Was it not appalling that no protest was filed by the university in 1943 when seven of its students and one professor were hanged after a farcical trial before the notorious Nazi judge, Roland Freisler?

The heroism of this small group of students is the one bright spot in the record of the universities during the Hitler regime. It seems to be the only example of an organized resistance cell within the academic community. Its story has been well told by the sister of the two leaders, Inge Aicher-Scholl,[56] and it is clear from her reflections that Hans and Sophie took their brave stand not because of their university education, but in spite of it. In an interview in 1972, she spoke of their home in Ulm where her "liberal father" and "pious mother" gave them a strong family sense of right and wrong. She recalls that they were little influenced by the general nationalistic atmosphere of the university, but instead read widely and were impressed by the natural-law theory of Thomas Aquinas, especially as they found it in Jacques Maritain. They also were close

[54]Letter from Karl Vossler to Kultusministerium, 13 July 1943, Vossler file, University of Munich Archives.

[55]Speech of Vossler, 2 November 1946, *Gedenkrede für die Opfer an der Universität München* (München: Pflaum Verlag, 1947) 17.

[56]Inge Scholl, *Die Weisse Rose* (Frankfurt am Main: Verlag der Frankfürter Hefte, 1952). Interview with the author, Ulm, January 1972. Other works that deal with the Scholl group are James Donohoe, *Hitler's Conservative Opponents in Bavaria, 1930-1945* (Leiden: E. J. Brill, 1961) and Heike Bretschneider, "Der Widerstand gegen den Nationalsozialismus in Munchen 1933 bis 1945" (dissertation, University of Munich, 1968).

to Theodore Haecker and Karl Muth and others who wrote for *Hochland*, a Catholic periodical. Whatever the cause of their clear-sightedness, the Scholls rejected the ideology of Nazism with strong words: "The day of reckoning has come, of reckoning between our German youth and the most abominable tyranny our nation has ever tolerated. In the name of the entire German people we demand back from the State of Adolf Hitler our personal freedom."[57] They wrote and distributed many pamphlets carrying such messages to the people around Munich. They denounced imperialism in all its forms, the hegemony of Prussia in the history of Germany, and called for a moderate socialism that would respect basic rights and liberties. They paid for their brave words with their lives.

The one faculty member included in the Scholl group was Professor Kurt Huber. Despite his active role in their work and his death at the hands of the Nazi regime, there are some ambiguities about his resistance. In the early days of the new order he was at the University of Berlin, but asked to be relieved of his work there when he was told to utilize music as a way of demonstrating the German *Völkisch* tradition; he saw this as a violation of his academic freedom. Yet in 1940 he joined the National Socialist party out of fear of communism.[58] He even accused the Nazis of being "too Leftist" and had serious disagreements with Hans Scholl on this point. Huber was the main author of the 7 February 1943 "Manifesto of the Munich Students" (which was to lead to their arrest), but his anti-Soviet exhortation in the draft of the statement was deleted by Scholl before publication.[59] It was just at the time of Stalingrad, and there was obviously a difference of opinion among the resisters as to whether or not the German defeat there was something to celebrate.

Huber also is puzzling because of his friendship with Karl Alexander von Müller, whose cooperation with the regime was well known. It may have been his strong anti-communist feelings that sometimes put him in strange company. For his association with the Scholls, he was executed. The University of Munich Senate stripped him of all academic honors prior to carrying out the

---

[57]Scholl, *Die Weisse Rose*, 108-10, for text of the pamphlets.

[58]Reference is made in several places to Huber's membership in the party, but I have not found any specific reason given for his joining it. Nor is it clear how he found his way into the Scholl group, which was formed about 1942. In any case, when on trial in 1943, he insisted to the court that his involvement with the Scholls was due to a deep sense of moral responsibility. See Arnold Bergstraesser, "Zum 20 Juli 1963," *Vierteljahrshefte für Zeitgeschichte* 12 (1964): 6.

[59]For a discussion of his relations with Hans Scholl, see Donohoe, *Hitler's Conservative Opponents*, 186.

sentence, thus making a public declaration that professors should not be counted among resisters.[60]

By 1943 such an action could have been predicted. The universities had shown that they had no stomach for conflict. Even Hitler recognized that, and while he expressed frustration at not being able to get the cooperation he desired from the churches, he often said that there was no such problem with the universities.[61] Inge Aicher-Scholl experienced a lack of sympathy when she and her family journeyed from Ulm to Munich to bury her sister and brother and were treated with disrespect and unpleasantness by the rector of the university. When they returned to Ulm, the whole family was imprisoned, and while some individual students expressed compassion, they were ignored by the academic community in general.[62]

The impact of this small group was minimal. Such incidents were never publicized and were spoken of locally in whispers, if at all. Albert Speer claimed that he would not even have known about it, although he was minister of armaments, except that he happened to hear the story through a friend who was in Munich.[63] It was only after the war that the university recognized the heroism of the group and named the street in front of the main building *Geschwister-Scholl Platz*. Until then the bright flame of freedom would remain extinguished in the German universities.

---

[60]Grunberger, *The 12-Year Reich*, 312-13.

[61]Albert Speer, interview, January 1972.

[62]Inge Aicher-Scholl, interview, January 1972.

[63]Speer interview.

Conclusion

The question I began with was "How were academia and politics related in pre-Hitler Germany?" This question arose from a study of German resistance movements during the Hitler period when it was discovered that, although there were "resisters" of one degree or another in labor unions, churches, the foreign office, and even the army, there was nothing comparable in the universities. Why not? There continues to be a deep puzzlement for historians—and for the general public—concerning Hitler's rise to power and the responsibility of the German people for such a tragedy. How was it possible, we keep asking, in a nation where learning and culture were so respected? How could people have stood by—seemingly helpless—as their country descended to the level of barbarism evidenced in the Third Reich?

The cause has been sought in economic depression, in a psychological predisposition on the part of the German people, in the creation of a political power vacuum by the kaiser's forced abdication. Without discounting any of these important circumstances, one must still look to the roles played by the different social institutions in the decisive period of the late Weimar Republic. Free decisions, made by individuals and by the groups to which they belonged, also played a significant part in the Hitler phenomenon. It is the contention of this study that most of the professors in the German universities in those years must bear a portion of the blame for the rise of National Socialism and for the German catastrophe that followed.

In the work of Baldwin and Goldthwaite, *Universities in Politics*, the same question of the relationship between the State and the academic community was raised regarding the early European universities: Paris, Bologna, Prague, Oxford, and Cambridge. The conclusion of these authors is that "the story of the university's entry into politics becomes that of the domination of the university by politics."[1] Having studied the history of the professors in the German universities during Weimar, I conclude that it is also true that if the

---

[1]John W. Baldwin and Richard A. Goldthwaite, eds., *Universities in Politics* (Baltimore: Johns Hopkins University Press, 1972) 15.

university refuses to enter the political life of the society in which it exists, it can also come to be dominated by politics.

It was the refusal to see political organization and activity as a necessary corollary of parliamentary democracy that permitted the professors to cherish their self-image as "above politics." Similarly, they refused to accept the social consequences of a university education which ignored the fact that *Bildung*, as originally understood, aimed at moral character as an inevitable by-product of "cultivation." What resulted was an educated citizenry that refused to accept responsibility for its own national government. Professor Wilhelm Hoffman, a distinguished librarian at the *Staatsbibliotek* in Stuttgart from 1931 to 1972, emphasized this point in a conversation with me in 1972. "We can say it was Fate," he remarked, "but that is absolutely unacceptable!" He insisted that if that were the case, history would be insoluble, without meaning. He claimed that the answer to the question about Hitler's rise to power could not be found in the moment when it happened, but "long, long before." Bismarck had made all the decisions and had taken from the people their ability to arrange their own affairs—hence they lost their sense of responsibility. Above all, he claimed it was education that had failed. By that word, "education," he meant the family, the school, the church, the parties, the universities. There was a sadness in the way that Professor Hoffman and other retired professors spoke of the failure of their own generation in this matter.

On 26 April 1926 a small group from the university faculties—led by Meinecke, Radbruch, and Kahl—had attempted to unite the professors behind the Republic. They urged their colleagues to put aside their personal longing for the "old times" and give leadership to the new political order. The response was disappointing.

On 7 April 1933 the academic community received its mandate for *Gleichschaltung* with the promulgation of the "Law on the Reorganization of the Career Public Service." From this time on the professors were, in fact, just one more channel through which the will of the Führer was communicated to the German people. Their treasured freedom to determine membership within their ranks was obliterated by a stroke of the pen; with that basic premise of academia violated, there was no longer any guarantee of freedom to teach and freedom to learn. The tradition of academic freedom, long associated with German universities, had been deteriorating within because of antisocialist, antidemocratic, and anti-Semitic prejudice; it was killed on 7 April 1933.

Between these two Aprils, 1926 and 1933, the political fate of Germany had been determined. It is true that very few professors were active members of the National Socialist party before 1933. Nevertheless, by their nationalist ideology, their aversion to politics, and their obstinate refusal to reform the universities themselves, they did assist in the "birthing" process of National Socialism. They were the "midwives" of the new order.

One can summarize their contributions as midwives under three headings: rhetoric; educational philosophy and practice; and clinging to a self-image as "unpolitical" while, in reality, being strongly antidemocratic.

Rhetoric. An analysis of the speeches delivered by the rectors on the occasion of the anniversary of the Foundation of the Reich uncovered the same concepts and language that were later heard in the speeches of Hitler and Goebbels. Idealization of the German *Volk*, of the *Reich*, of the *Einheit* of the German nation despite the geographic boundaries drawn up at Versailles, of the hero who would be *der Führer*—all these were the idiom in which they spoke and wrote. The counterpoint to these glorious ideals was found in Weimar, Versailles, cultural bolshevism, weakness of parliamentary leaders, democratization of life. The speeches on *Partaitag* in Speer's stadium at Nuremburg did not sound strange or innovative to the ears of a generation reared on such rhetoric. Although most of the attendees at such gatherings may not have been university graduates, they had all been affected by teachers trained in this tradition.

It may be argued that although the words used by Hitler and by the professors were the same, the meaning was different. While this may be true, the burden of proof rests on those who would defend the professors' language. Precision of language has long been claimed as one of the gifts of the scholar. The care of language and the transmission of it to another generation is one of the most serious duties of the teacher. The "habit of mind," which was the goal of the university as described by Newman, included this respect for the accurate use of words:

> I say that one main portion of intellectual education, of the labours of both school and university, is to remove the original dimness of the mind's eye; to strengthen and perfect its vision; to enable it to look out into the world right forward, steadily and truly; to give the mind clearness, accuracy, precision; to enable it to use words aright, to understand what it says, to conceive justly what it thinks about, to abstract, compare, analyze, divide, define, and reason correctly.[2]

Can the professors be absolved of responsibility for the illusions of German grandeur that their rhetoric evoked? Can they deny that their choice of words supported a vision of Germany totally out of touch with the political realities? Would they not have to admit that the Nazis would have had a more difficult time arousing the fervor of German youth if the students had been nourished on a different vocabulary: international conciliation; human rights; individual

---

[2]John Henry Newman, *The Idea of a University* (New York: Doubleday Image, 1959) 312-13.

conscience; equal opportunity for education and leadership; dignity of every human person? These were the concepts urged upon the professors at the Weimar meeting in April 1926—the kind of principles on which the republic had been founded. But the rhetoric of the professors was untouched by them.

Educational philosophy. A second way in which the professors acted as midwives to National Socialism was in their understanding of university education itself. In examining the thought of Fichte and Humboldt, I noted the link that they perceived between humanistic education and social responsibility. In their educational philosophy both ethics and politics were related to intellectual development and were essential to a liberal education. Fichte's concept of *Kulturmission,* without its later connotations of nationalism and romanticism, required an education that prepared young people for leadership in the State. He explained how the cultivation of the "things of the mind" would lead those so educated to serve their nation well. There was in his ideal university a strong emphasis on "synthesis" of knowledge and on integrity of life.

However, the developments in nineteenth-century German universities moved in another direction. Analysis rather than synthesis was the key. Positivistic criteria were sought in every discipline, even philosophy and theology. A narrow specialization became essential for the professor who wished to be regarded as a scholar of significance. Training for the professions, always a remote goal of university education, became the top priority. Professors became a class apart, seemingly locked into library and laboratory.

This image of the German professor became the target of groups of romantic and nationalistic writers of the late nineteenth century. These professors were often denounced as "un-German" and censured for being uninterested in new currents of thought, particularly in what could be learned from the "cult of personality." Reacting to this criticism, the universities became the bastion of the "rational" and gloried in their image as ivory towers where discipline-oriented research held sway and where no effort was made to relate the world of the university to the world around it. Their language, ironically, continued to mimic that of Fichte. They explained their isolation in terms of *Wissenschaft,* of the scholar's need for quiet and freedom from political concerns, and of the overwhelming task of preparing the next generation of "culture-bearers" for the German nation.

It was in carrying out this task that the educational philosophy of the twentieth-century professors merged in some important ways with the current of thought outside the university known as the Conservative Revolution. In chapter 2 I dealt at length with the efforts of these journalists and publicists to destroy once and for all the "ideas of 1789"—liberty, equality, fraternity. Seen as diametrically opposed to the German "ideas of 1914," these goals of 1789 were denounced. Naturally, the Weimar Republic was seen as an attempt by the victorious West to impose such foreign and un-German concepts on a nation with quite a different mission—the cultural triumph of the Third Reich.

While the professors were not, in any visible way, connected with the Conservative Revolution, they fought off some of the criticism leveled against them by trying to outdo the publicists in their devotion to the same values. Just as they gave way to the demands of the specialists while continuing to reiterate the phrases of Fichte about humanistic education, so they accepted and used the concepts of *Reich*, *Führer*, and *Kulturstaat* being disseminated by Moeller van den Bruck and his friends without losing their self-image as "above politics."

The cultural purposes of the State were uppermost in the minds of the university educators. Friedrich Meinecke's nuanced explanation of how to distinguish the modern State from the medieval "German nation" went unheeded. Instead the professors dedicated themselves to inspiring their students with a deep love for the Fatherland, a hatred for Versailles and all it stood for (including the ideas of 1789), an idolatry of the "true German spirit," and a firm belief in the cultural unity of all Germans—a unity that would find its new home in a new Reich under a new leader.

One would need to do a longitudinal/psychological study of the students during this era (1925-1933) to discover whether or not they adopted the language and political attitudes of their teachers. Steinberg suggests that the students saw themselves as "above politics," a phrase long associated with the leaders of academia.[3] One would not want either to overestimate the impact of the professors or to dismiss their influence too lightly.

Another relevant facet of the professors' educational philosophy was their opposition to any enlargement of the student body. The Weimar government attempted to provide places in the university for all who qualified. Traditionally, the possession of the *Abitur* followed completion of the course in a Gymnasium and was thus the ticket to university study. But now alternative secondary schools were developing, the *Abitur* was being distributed more widely, and the universities were becoming overcrowded. The professors found in this one more complaint against the Weimar Republic and its democratizing tendencies. They strongly resisted such "reforms."

This negative attitude toward expansion of educational opportunity was consistent with their antidemocratic view of the German State. The State could only carry out its function of "bearing" the culture of the German people if the persons who led it were educated in the traditional "humanistic" way. A State, furthermore, that depended for its legitimacy on the will of the people could

---

[3]Michael Stephen Steinberg, *Sabers and Brown Shirts* (Chicago: University of Chicago Press, 1977) 72-73.

never be a true instrument for the German nation, whose mission was rooted in the Kingdom of God, the prototype of the Reich.

One sees the professors paying lip service to the great ideals of the university while, at the same time, undermining these ideals in their operational educational programs and decisions. An education based on such nationalistic and antidemocratic attitudes proved to be no dike to hold back the tide of National Socialism. Rather, it opened the locks and unleashed the deluge.

Political theory and practice. The professors, then, conceived of the State as an instrument through which the cultural union already existing in the *Volk* could act. Turning their backs on the social-contract theory and other "Western" understandings of the relationship between the people and the State, these academics clung to a notion of nation that preceded and transcended the State and also was rooted not in geographic or political boundaries but in blood and tradition.

Their speeches give clear evidence of their antidemocratic positions. There is no talk of individual rights, only talk of the needs of the nation. The authoritarian organization and structure of the university itself—that is, a small group of full professors governing it—suited them well. Their recollection of the brief period of parliamentary government in 1848 was an unhappy one. The weaknesses they perceived in the postwar leadership only confirmed them in their views. The perceived inability of the Weimar government to control inflation, fight unemployment, or protect the country against the Communist threat bolstered their argument. By their education and in light of their experience, the professors favored the parties on the Right side of the political spectrum. While insisting that they were "above politics," they nonetheless had little tolerance for political dissent within the community. The cases of Gumbel and Nawiasky, which I have used as illustrations of this intolerance, indicate a great aversion to socialists, pacifists, and Jews within the academic community. The refusal of the professors to defend their colleagues against such charges was explained by the need they saw to be "in harmony" with the *Volk* and the *Kultur*. Freedom to think differently from one's peers was not a value if it led one to sympathize with Western artists, musicians, or social scientists. Nor was it operative if a member of the academic community professed pacifist or socialist views. Jews were regarded as "un-German" or "outsiders" by many, and their support for the Weimar Republic gave the professors another reason to be against it.

The law of 7 April 1933 on reorganizing the civil service ended any ambiguity in this regard. No longer were Jews eligible for appointment to university teaching posts; moreover, those already there would be dismissed. Was there an uproar from academia? Was this interference with their prerogatives denounced? Unfortunately not. Their own thinking had prepared the way for such an edict. The lack of protest speaks volumes. The year 1933 was not like 1943, when all dissent was punishable by death. One can only conclude that the professors saw no need to protest.

The way the professors viewed the State made any kind of resistance or nonconformity unthinkable for them. There was no support in the German intellectual tradition for the concept of civil disobedience or active resistance to a legitimate government. Yet other groups in these early days of Hitler's government presented many oral and written protests. Why didn't the professors confront Berlin on this law, which so clearly discriminated against their Jewish colleagues? Had they no sense of responsibility for the injustice done thereby?

Finally, then, one is faced with an inevitable conclusion. When Hitler came to power academia refused to accept its proper responsibilities. The professors sought refuge from the specter of a tyrannical Third Reich, both physically in their retreat to their studies and psychologically in their insistence that politics was not their proper sphere of influence and activity. Were they only "guilty bystanders" or mere "precursors" of the Nazi takeover? From one point of view they can be exonerated by claiming that whatever they had done, it would have made little difference. There might still have been a Third Reich and a Holocaust.

The lesson one can learn, however, from the German experience is that academia and politics cannot be divorced that easily. It is impossible in the twentieth century—given our dependence on institutional structures—for an institution to be politically neutral. Silence has its own price, and both personal and social ethics require moral decision. Individual consciences are formed by a variety of influences: home, family, neighborhood, church, school, friends, media, etc. By focusing on the responsibility of university professors, I am not suggesting that theirs is the only significant role in the educative process. But it has to be an important one or it loses its own reason for being. In his study of the Third Reich, Bracher points to this factor:

> Education and scholarship may capitulate to seductions and manipulations which pave the way for a regime like Hitler's—if the political passivity of the educated stratum is responsive to the tendencies which flourished in the partly unpolitical, partly undemocratic atmosphere of the German schools and universities. What proved fatal were not only the crimes of a National Socialist minority and its petty bourgeois fellow travelers but also the failure of a majority of the "educated."[4]

If those who devote themselves to a life of research and teaching see no relationship between the truth they seek and the contribution they can and should make to their society, then the other social institutions cannot be blamed if they regard academia as irrelevant to the decision-making processes. Above all, the

---

[4] Karl Dietrich Bracher, *The German Dictatorship* (New York: Praeger, 1970) 443.

integrity of the university depends on the way in which it carries out its own mission of mediating the best of human tradition to a new generation. Such mediation requires critical judgments of the past as well as fidelity to tradition; it demands minds open to new values and new realities.

Had the professors realized that they could not be "above politics" by simply willing to be so, they might have forced themselves to come to terms with the proper role of their universities at such a moment of crisis. Instead they clung to outmoded patterns of thought and action, strengthening the myths and undermining the political process; and in this disowning of the present and the future, they facilitated the birth of the Third Reich. In this lay the tragedy, for without desiring it or intending it, they became the midwives for Hitler. Like Speer, they probably never fully could understand the role they played.

Bibliography

Books and Dissertations

Adam, Karl. *Christ and the Western Mind*. Translated by Edward Bullough. New York: Macmillan Co., 1930.

Albertin, Lothar. *Liberalismus und Demokratie am Anfang der Weimarer Republik*. Dusseldorf: Droste Verlag, 1972.

Almond, Gabriel. *The Struggle for Democracy in Germany*. Chapel Hill: University of North Carolina Press, 1949.

Aris, Reinhold. *History of Political Thought in Germany*. New York: Russell & Russell Inc., 1965.

Baldwin, John W. and Richard A. Goldthwaite, eds. *Universities in Politics*. Baltimore: Johns Hopkins University Press, 1972.

Baumgardt, David. *Looking back on a German University Career*. An offprint of *Yearbook 10* of Leo Baeck Institute. London, 1965.

Baumgarten, Eduard. *Zustand und Zukunft der deutschen Universität*. Tübingen: J. C. B. Mohr, 1963.

Bayles, William. *Seven Were Hanged*. London: Gollancz, 1945.

Baynes, Norman H., ed. *The Speeches of Adolf Hitler*. Volume one (April 1922-August 1939). New York: Oxford University Press, 1942.

Becker, Carl Heinrich. *Ein Gedenkbuch*. Göttingen: Vandenhoeck & Ruprecht, 1950.

Berlau, Abraham Joseph. *The German Social Democratic Party, 1914-1921*. New York: Octagon, 1970.

Besson, Waldemar. *Württemberg und die deutsche Staatskrise, 1928-1933*. Stuttgart: Deutsche Verlags-Anstalt, 1959.

Beyerchen, Alan D. *Scientists under Hitler: Politics and the Physics Community in the Third Reich*. New Haven: Yale University Press, 1977.

Beyerle, Konrad. *Zehn Jahre Reichsverfassung*. München: Max Hüber, 1929.

Bleul, Hans Peter. *Deutschlands Bekenner Professoren zwischen Kaiserreich und Diktatur*. München: Scherz, 1968.

_____ and A. Klimert. *Deutsche Studenten auf dem Weg ins Dritte Reich*. Gütersloh: Mohr, 1967.

Bossenbrook, William J. *The German Mind*. Detroit: Wayne State University Press, 1961.

Bracher, Karl Dietrich. *Die Auflösung der Weimarer Republik*. Villingen/Schwarzwald: Ring Verlag, 1960.

_____. *Deutschland zwischen Demokratie und Diktatur: Beiträge zur neueren Politik und Geschichte*. München: Scherz, 1964.

_____. *The German Dictatorship*. New York: Praeger, 1970.

_____. *Die nationalsozialistische Machtergreifung*. Köln: Opladen, 1960.

Breitman, Richard. *German Socialism and Weimar Democracy*. Chapel Hill: University of North Carolina Press, 1981.

Bretschneider, Heike. *Der Widerstand gegen den Nationalsozialismus in München 1933 bis 1945*. München: Stadtarchiv, 1968.

Breuning, Klaus. *Die Vision des Reiches. Deutscher Katholizimus zwischen Demokratie und Diktatur, 1929-1934*. München: Max Hüber Verlag, 1969.

Bruford, W. H. *The German Tradition of Self-Cultivation*. New York: Cambridge University Press, 1975.

Buchheim, Hans. *The Third Reich*. London: Oswald Wolff, 1961.

Buchheim, Karl. *Die Weimarer Republik*. London: Oswald Wolff, 1970.

Busch, Alexander. *Die Geschichte des Privatozenten: Eine soziologische Studie zur grossbetrieblichen Entwicklung der deutschen Universitäten*, in H. Plessner, ed., *Göttinger Abhandlungen zur Sociologie 5*. Stuttgart, 1959.

Carmon, Arye Zvi. "The University of Heidelberg and National Socialism." Dissertation, University of Wisconsin, 1974.

Craig, John E. *Scholarship and Nation Building. The Universities of Strasbourg and Alsatian Society, 1870-1939*. Chicago: University of Chicago Press, 1984.

Deak, Istvan. *Weimar Germany's Left-Wing Intellectuals*. Berkeley: University of California Press, 1968.

Deutsch, Harold C. *The Conspiracy against Hitler*. Minneapolis: The University of Minnesota Press, 1968.

Deutsches Geistesleben und National-Sozialismus: Eine Vortragsreihe der Universität Tübingen. Tübingen: Flitner, 1965.

Doeberl, Michael. *Das Akademische Deutschland*. Four vols. Berlin: C. A. Weller, 1930-1931.

Donohoe, James. *Hitler's Conservative Opponents in Bavaria, 1930-1945*. Leiden: E. J. Brill, 1961.

Döring, Herbert. *Der Weimarer Kreis*. Meisenheim: Verlag Anton Hain, 1975.

Drobisch, Klaus. *Wir schweigen Nicht.* Berlin: Union Verlag, 1968.

Encyclopedia Britannica. Volume twenty-two. "Universitas," 745-67. Chicago: William Benton, 1971.

Engelbrecht, Helmuth Carl. *Johann Gottlieb Fichte.* New York: AMS Press, 1968.

Epstein, Fritz, ed. *Minerva: Jahrbuch der gelehrten Welt.* Berlin: Walter de Gruyter & Co., 1930.

Epstein, Klaus. *The Genesis of German Conservatism.* Princeton: Princeton University Press, 1966.

Eschenburg, Theodor. *Die improvisierte Demokratie.* München: Piper, 1963.

_____. *Der Weg in die Diktator 1918 bis 1933.* München: Piper, 1963.

Evans, Ellen Lowell. *The German Center Party, 1870-1933.* Carbondale IL: Southern Illinois University Press, 1981.

Eyck, Erich. *A History of the Weimar Republic,* vols. 1 and 2. Translated by Harlan P. Hanson and Robert G. L. Waite. New York: Atheneum, 1970.

Fallon, Daniel. *The German University.* Boulder CO: Associated University Press, 1980.

Faust, Anselm. "Studenten und Nationalsozialismus in der Weimarer Republik: Der Nationalsozialistische Deutsche Studentenbund." Dissertation, Ludwig-Maximilians-Universität, 1971. Published as *Der Nationalsozialistische Deutsche Studentenbund: Studenten und Nationalsozialismus in der Weimarer Republik.* Two vols. Dusseldorf: Padagogischer Verlag Schwann, 1973.

Ferber, Christian von. *Die Entwicklung des Lehrkörpers der deutschen Universitäten und Hochschulen, 1864-1954.* Göttingen: Vandenhoeck & Ruprecht, 1956.

Fichte, Johann Gottlieb. *Addresses to the German Nation.* New York: Harper and Row, 1968.

_____. *Reden an die deutsche Nation.* München: J. F. Lehmann, 1929.

_____. *Sämmtliche Werke.* Bd. 8. Edited by J. H. Fichte. Berlin: Veit and Co., 1845.

Fischer, Fritz. *Germany's Aims in the First World War.* New York: W. W. Norton, 1967.

Fleming, Donald and Bernard Bailyn, eds. *The Intellectual Migration.* Cambridge MA: Harvard University Press, 1969.

Flexner, Abraham. *Universities: American, English, German.* New York: Oxford University Press, 1930.

Franz, Ludwig. "Der politische Kampf an den Münchener Hochschulen von 1929 bis 1933 im Spiegel der Presse." Dissertation, University of München, 1949.

Fraser, Lindley. *Germany between Two Wars. A Study of Propaganda and War Guilt.* New York: Oxford University Press, 1945.

Friedlander, Henry and Sybil Milton, eds. *The Holocaust: Ideology, Bureaucracy, and Genocide*. Millwood NY: Kraus International Publications, 1980.

Frings, Manfred S. *Max Scheler*. Pittsburgh: Duquesne University Press, 1965.

Gallin, Mary Alice, O.S.U. *The German Resistance to Hitler: Ethical and Religious Factors*. Washington: The Catholic University of America Press, 1955.

Gay, Peter. *Weimar Culture. The Outsider as Insider*. New York: Harper and Row, 1968.

Gerhart, Walter (pseudonym for W. Gurian). *Um des Reiches Zukunft, Nationale Wiedergeburt oder politische Reaktion?* Freiburg, 1932.

Goetz, Walter. *Historiker in Meiner Zeit*. Köln: Bohlan, 1957.

Gotz, Frhr v. Polnitz. *Denkmale und Dokumente zur Geschichte der Ludwig-Maximilians Universität. Ingolstadt-Landshut-München*. University Archives, 1942.

Gopalakrishnaiah, U. *A Comparative Study of the Educational Philosophies of J. G. Fichte and J. H. Newman*. Waltair: Andhra University Press, 1973.

Greive, Hermann. *Theologie und Ideologie: Katholizimus und Judentum in Deutschland und Österreich*. Heidelberg: Verlag Lambert Schneider, 1969.

Grunberger, Richard. *The 12-Year Reich*. New York: Holt, Rinehart and Winston, 1971.

Guardini, R. *Die Waage des Daseins. Gedachtnisrede auf die Geschwister Scholl*. Tübingen: Wunderlich, 1946.

Gumbel, Emil, ed. *Freie Wissenschaft*. Strasbourg: Sebastian Brant, 1938.

_____. *Verschwörer*. Wien: Malik Verlag, 1924.

Haller, Johannes. *England und Deutschland in die Jahrhundertwende*. Leipzig: Quelle und Meyer, 1929.

_____. *Epochen der deutschen Geschichte*. Stuttgart: J. G. Cotta, 1923, 1939, 1950.

_____. *Lebenserrinnerungen*. Stuttgart: Kohlhammer, 1960.

_____. *Tausend Jahre deutsch-französischer Beziehungen*. Stuttgart: J. G. Cotta, 1930.

Halperin, S. William. *Germany Tried Democracy: A Political History of the Reich from 1918 to 1933*. New York: Thomas Y. Crowell Co., 1946.

Hartshorne, Edward Yarnall. *The German Universities and National Socialism*. Cambridge MA: Harvard University Press, 1937.

Heiber, Helmut. *Walter Frank und sein Reichsinstitut für Geschichte des neuen Deutschlands*. Stuttgart: Deutsches Verlags Anstalt, 1966.

Heinemann, Ulrich. *Die verdrängte Niederlage. Politische Offentlichkeit und Kriegschuldfrage in der Weimarer Republik*. Göttingen: Vandenhoeck & Ruprecht, 1983.

Helmreich, Ernst Christian. *The German Churches under Hitler*. Detroit: Wayne State University Press, 1979.

Hertzman, Lewis. *DNVP: Right-Wing Opposition in the Weimar Republic*. Lincoln: University of Nebraska Press, 1963.

Herzfeld, Hans. "Deutsche Geschichtsschreibung der Weimarer Zeit," in *Ausgewählte Aufsätze*. Berlin: Walter de Gruyter, 1962.

Hess, Gerhard. *Die deutsche Universität, 1930-1970*. Bad Godesberg: Inter Nationes, 1968.

Heyse, H. *Die Idee der Wissenschaft und die deutsche Universität*. Konigsberg, 1933.

Hitler, Adolf. *My New Order*. New York: Reynal and Hitchcock, 1941.

Hoffman, Peter. *The History of the German Resistance, 1933-1945*. Cambridge MA: MIT Press, 1977.

Hoffman, Wilhelm. *Nach der Katastrophe*. Tübingen: R. Wunderlich, 1946.

Holborn, Hajo. *A History of Modern Germany, 1840-1945*. New York: Alfred A. Knopf, 1969.

_____, ed. *Republic to Reich*. Translated by Ralph Mannheim. New York: Pantheon Books, 1972.

Huber, Clara, ed. *Kurt Huber zum Gedächtnis*. Regensburg: Josef Habbel, 1947.

de Huszar, George B., ed. *The Intellectuals: a Controversial Portrait*. Glencoe: Free Press, 1960.

Iggers, George G. *The German Conception of History*. Wesleyan CT: Wesleyan University Press, 1968.

Jansen, Christian. *Der "Fall Gumbel" und die Heidelberger Universität, 1924-1932*. Heidelberg, 1981.

Jarausch, Konrad H. *Students, Society, and Politics in Imperial Germany*. Princeton: Princeton University Press, 1982.

_____. *The Transformation of Higher Learning, 1860-1930*. Chicago: University of Chicago Press, 1983.

Jaspers, Karl. *Die geistige Situation der Zeit*. Berlin: Walter de Gruyter & Co., 1947.

_____. *Die Idee der Universität*. Berlin: Springer, 1961.

_____. *The Question of German Guilt*. New York: Dial Press, 1947.

Kahl, Wilhelm, Friedrich Meinecke, and Gustav Radbruch. *Die deutschen Universitäten und der heutige Staat*. Tübingen: J. C. B. Mohr, 1926.

Kahle, Paul. *Bonn University in Pre-Nazi and Nazi Times*. London: privately printed, 1945.

_____. *Die deutsche Universität im Dritten Reich*. München, 1966.

Kasper, G., H. Huber, K. Kaebsch, and Fr. Senger, eds. *Die Hochschulverwaltung.* Two vols. Berlin, 1942/3.

Kater, Michael. *Studentenschaft und Rechtsradikalismus im Deutschland, 1918-1933.* Hamburg: Hoffman und Campe Verlag, 1975.

Kaufmann, Walter H. *Monarchism in the Weimar Republic.* New York: Bookman Associates, 1953.

Kelly, Reece Conn. "National Socialism and German University Teachers: The NSDAP's Efforts to Create a National Socialist Professoriate and Scholarship." Dissertation, University of Washington, 1973.

Klemperer, Klemens von. *Germany's New Conservatism.* Princeton: Princeton University Press, 1957.

Kluge, Alexander. *Die Universitätsselbstverwaltung. Ihre Geschichte und Gegenwärtige Rechtsform.* Frankfurt, 1958.

Koehler, Wolfgang. *The Task of Gestalt Psychology.* Princeton: Princeton University Press, 1969.

Königsberger Universitätsreden, #5. Königsberg: Hartungsche Buchdruckerei, 1929.

Kotschnig, Walter M. and Elined Prys, eds. *The University in a Changing World.* Freeport, New York: Books for Libraries Press, 1932.

Krieger, Leonard. *The German Idea of Freedom.* Boston: Beacon Press, 1957.

Kuhn, Helmut, ed. *Die deutsche Universität im Dritten Reich.* München: R. Piper & Co., 1966.

_____. *Freedom Forgotten and Remembered.* Chapel Hill: University of North Carolina Press, 1943.

Langsam, Walter Consuelo. *Documents and Readings in the History of Europe since 1918.* New York: J. B. Lippincott Co., 1939.

Lilge, Frederic. *The Abuse of Learning.* New York: The Macmillan Co., 1948.

Lutz, Heinrich. *Demokratie im Zwielicht. Der Weg der deutschen Katholiken aus dem Kaiserreich in die Republik, 1914-1925.* München, 1963.

Lutz, R. H. *Causes of the German Collapse.* Stanford: University of Stanford Press, 1934.

_____. *The Fall of the German Empire, 1914-1918.* Two vols. Stanford: University of Stanford Press, 1932.

Mann, Erika and Klaus Mann. *Escape to Freedom.* Boston: Houghton Mifflin Co., 1939.

Mann, Thomas. *Deutsche Ansprache.* Berlin: S. Fischer Verlag, 1930.

_____. *The Magic Mountain.* Translated by H. T. Lowe-Porter. New York: Heritage Press, 1962.

Matthias, Erich and Rudolf Morsey, eds. *Das Ende der Parteien 1933*. Dusseldorf: Droste Verlag, 1960.

Mayer, J. P. *Max Weber and German Politics*. London: Faber and Faber Ltd., 1944.

Meinecke, Friedrich. *The German Catastrophe*. Cambridge MA: Harvard University Press, 1950.

_____. *Nach der Revolution: Geschichtliche Betrachtungen über unsere Lage*. Berlin: R. Oldenbourgh, 1919.

_____. *Werke*, bd. 6. Stuttgart: Dehio und Classen, 1962.

Mennekes, Friedhelm. *Die Republik als Herausforderung*. Berlin: Duncker und Humblot, 1972.

Moehling, Karl A. "Martin Heidegger and the Nazi Party: An Examination." Dissertation, Northern Illinois University, 1972.

Moeller van den Bruck, Arthur. *Germany's Third Empire*. Translated by E. O. Lorimer. London: G. Allen and Unwin, 1934.

Mohler, Armin. *Die Konservative Revolution in Deutschland, 1918-1932*. Stuttgart: F. Vorwerk, 1952.

Mosse, George. *The Crisis of German Ideology*. New York: Grosset and Dunlap, 1964.

_____. *Germans and Jews*. New York: Grosset and Dunlap, 1970.

Nawiasky, Hans. *Die Munchener Universitätskrawalle*. München, 1931.

_____. *Die Stellung des Berufsbeamtentums im parlamentarischen Staat*. München, 1926.

_____. *Die Zukunft der politischen Parteien*. München, 1924.

Newman, John Henry. *The Idea of a University*. New York: Doubleday Image, 1959.

Nicholls, Anthony and Erich Matthias, eds. *German Democracy and the Triumph of Hitler*. New York: St. Martin's Press, 1972.

_____. *Weimar and the Rise of Hitler*. New York: The Macmillan Co., 1968.

Oncken, Hermann. *Nation und Geschichte, Reden und Aufsätze, 1919-1935*. Berlin, 1935.

_____. "Die Weltgeschichtliche Keimzelle des Kriegschuldproblems," in *Die Grosse Politik der Europäischen Kabinette, 1871-1914*, bd. 40. Arbeitsausschuss Deutsche Verbinde, 1927.

Paulsen, Friedrich. *The German Universities and University Study*. Translated by Frank Thilly and Wm. W. Elwang. New York: C. Scribner's Sons, 1906.

Pinson, Koppel S. *Modern Germany*. New York: The Macmillan Co., 1966.

Pois, Robert. "Friedrich Meinecke and German Politics in the Twentieth Century." Dissertation, University of Wisconsin, 1965.

Prahl, Hans Werner and Ingrid Schmidt-Haybach. *Die Universität*. München: C. J. Bucher, 1981.

Pross, Helge. *Die Deutsche Akademische Emigration nach den Vereinigten Staaten, 1933-1941*. Berlin, 1955.

Radbruch, Gustav. *Der innere Weg: Anfriss meines Lebens*. Stuttgart, 1951.

Ranly, Ernst W., C.P.P.S. *Scheler's Phenomenology of Community*. The Hague: Martinus Nijhoff, 1966.

Rashdall, Hastings. *The Universities of Europe in the Middle Ages*. Two vols. Edited by F. M. Powicke and A. B. Emden. Oxford: The Clarendon Press, 1936.

Rein, A. *Die Idee der politischen Universität*. Hamburg, 1933.

Reiss, H. S. *The Political Thought of the German Romantics*. Oxford: Blackwell, 1955.

Rhodes, James Michael. "The Conservative Revolution in Germany: Myths of Contracted Reality." Dissertation, University of Notre Dame, 1969.

Richter, Werner. *Wissenschaft und Geist in der Weimarer Republik*. Köln: Opladen Westdtsch, 1958.

_____. *Die Zukunft der deutschen Universität*. Marburg/Lahn: Simons Verlag, 1949.

Ringer, Fritz K. *The Decline of the German Mandarins*. Cambridge MA: Harvard University Press, 1969.

Ritter, Gerhard. *The German Problem*. Columbus: Ohio State University Press, 1965.

_____. *Die Idee der Universität und das öffentliche Leben*. Freiburg im Br.: 1946.

Ritterbusch, Paul. *Die deutsche Universität und der deutsche Geist*. Neumünster: K. Wachholtz, 1939.

The Road to Dictatorship, 1918-1933. London: Oswald Wolff, 1964.

Rochfahl, Felix. *Der Fall Valentin: Die amtlichen Urkunden*. München, 1920.

von Roon, Ger. *Neuordnung im Widerstand*. München: R. Oldenbourgh, 1967.

Ropke, Wilhelm. *The Solution of the German Problem*. Translated by E. W. Dickes. London: Geo. Allen and Unwin Ltd., 1946.

Rothfels, Hans. *Gerhard Ritter*, vol. 9 of *Reden Gedenkworte*. Heidelberg: Lambert Schneider, 1968-1969.

Samuel, Richard H. and R. Hinton Thomas. *Education and Society in Modern Germany*. 1949; rpt., Westport CT: Greenwood Press, 1971.

Scheler, Max. *On the Eternal in Man*. Translated by Bernard Noble. New York: Harper and Brothers, 1961.

Schilpp, Paul. *The Philosophy of Karl Jaspers*. New York: Tudor Publishing Co., 1957.

Scholl, Inge. *Die Weisse Rose*. Frankfurt am Main: Verlag der Frankfürter Hefte, 1952.

Schorske, Carl E. *German Social Democracy, 1905-1917*. Cambridge MA: Harvard University Press, 1955.

Schultze, Walter. *Grundfragen der deutschen Universität und Wissenschaft*. Neumünster: Wachholtz, 1938.

Schwend, Karl. *Bayern zwischen Monarchie und Diktatur*. München, 1954.

Sontheimer, Kurt. *Antidemokratisches Denken in der Weimarer Republik*. München: Nymphenburger, 1962.

_____. *Thomas Mann und die Deutschen*. München: Nymphenburger, 1961.

Speer, Albert. *Inside the Third Reich*. Translated by Richard Winston and Clara Winston. New York: The Macmillan Co., 1970.

Spengler, Oswald. *Neubau des Deutschen Reiches*. München: Beck, 1924.

_____. *Politische Schriften*. München: Beck, 1933.

Spranger, Eduard. *Das humanistische und das politische Bildungsideal im heutigen Deutschland*. Berlin, 1916.

Staude, John Raphael. *Max Scheler*. New York: The Free Press, 1967.

Steinberg, Michael Stephen. *Sabers and Brown Shirts*. Chicago: University of Chicago Press, 1977.

Sterling, Richard W. *Ethics in a World of Power*. Princeton: Princeton University Press, 1958.

Stern, Fritz. *The Failure of Illiberalism*. New York: Knopf, 1972.

_____. *The Politics of Cultural Despair*. Berkeley: University of California Press, 1961.

Stirk, Samuel Dickinson. *German Universities through English Eyes*. London: V. Gollanez Ltd., 1946.

Stone, Lawrence. *The University in Society*. Princeton: Princeton University Press, 1974.

Struve, Walter. *Elites against Democracy*. Princeton: Princeton University Press, 1974.

Sweet, Paul R. *Wilhelm von Humboldt: A Biography*. Two vols. Columbus: Ohio State University Press, 1980.

Tobler, Douglas. "German Historians and the Weimar Republic." Dissertation, University of Kansas, 1967.

Töpner, Kurt. *Gelehrte Politiker und politisierende Gelehrte.* Göttingen: Musterschmidt, 1970.

Trendelenburg, Wilhelm. *Festrede gehalten zur 450 Jahrfeier der Universität Tübingen beim Festakt in der Stiftskirche am 25 Juli 1927.* Tübingen, 1927.

Universitätstage 1966. Nationalsozialismus und die deutsche Universität. Berlin: Walter de Gruyter & Co., 1966.

Vermeil, Edmond. *Germany in the Twentieth Century.* New York: Praeger, 1956.

Voegelin, Eric. *The New Science of Politics.* Chicago: University of Chicago Press, 1952.

Waite, Robert G. L. *Vanguard of Nazism. The Free Corps Movement in Postwar Germany, 1918-1923.* Cambridge MA: Harvard University Press, 1952.

Weber, Max. *Politics as a Vocation.* Translated by H. H. Gerth and C. Wright Mills. Philadelphia: Fortress Press, 1965.

Weinreich, Max. *Hitler's Professors: The Part of Scholarship in Germany's Crimes against the Jewish People.* New York: Yiddish Scientific Institute, 1946.

Weisbach, Werner. *Geist und Gewalt.* Wien: A. Schroll, 1956.

Weisz, Christoph. *Geschichtsauffassung und politisches Denken Münchener Historiker der Weimarer Zeit.* Berlin: Duncker & Humblot, 1970.

Wende, Erich. *C. H. Becker, Mensch und Politiker.* Stuttgart: Deutsche Verlags Anstalt, 1959.

Werner, Karl Ferdinand. *Das NS-Geschichtsbild und die deutsche Geschichtswissenschaft.* Stuttgart, 1967.

Wiechert, Ernst. *An die deutsche Jugend.* München, 1951.

Wilbrandt, Robert. *Ihr Glücklichen Augen. Lebenserinnerungen.* Stuttgart: Franz Mittelbach, 1947.

Periodicals

Ascher, Abraham. "Professors as Propagandists: the Politics of the *Kathedersozialisten.*" *Journal of Central European History* 23 (1963-1964): 282-302.

Becker, Howard. "Befuddled Germany: A Glimpse of Max Scheler." *American Sociological Review* 8 (April 1943): 207-11.

Bergstraesser, Arnold. "Zum 20 Juli 1963." *Vierteljahrshefte für Zeitgeschichte* 12 (1964): 1-12.

Besson, Waldemar. "Friedrich Meinecke und die Weimarer Republik." *Vierteljahrshefte für Zeitgeschichte* 7 (1959): 113-29.

Bussmann, Walter. "Politische Ideologien zwischen Monarchie und Weimarer Republik." *Historische Zeitschrift* 190 (1960): 55-77.

Chanady, Attila. "The Disintegration of the German National People's Party, 1924-1930." *Journal of Modern History* 39 (March 1967): 65-91.

Curtius, Ernst Robert. "Abbau der Bildung." *Neue Rundschau* 42 (1931): 339-53.

_____. "Die Universität als Idee und als Erfahrung." *Neue Rundschau* 43 (1932): 359-84.

Deuerlein, Ernst. "Das war Weimar." *Politische Meinung* 7 (1962): 83-86.

Döring, Herbert. "Deutsche Professoren zwischen Kaiserreich und Dritten Reich." *Neue Politische Literatur* 19 (1974): 340-52.

Engel, Josef. "Die deutschen Universitäten und die Geschichtswissenschaft." *Historische Zeitschrift* 189 (1959): 223-378.

Erdmann, Karl Dietrich. "Die Geschichte der Weimarer Republik als Problem der Wissenschaft." *Vierteljahrshefte für Zeitgeschichte* 3 (1955): 1-19.

Eschenburg, Theodor. "Die Rolle der Personlichkeit in der Krise der Weimarer Republik." *Vierteljahrshefte für Zeitgeschichte* 9:1 (1961): 1-29.

Fuller, L. W. "War of 1914 as Interpreted by German Intellectuals." *Journal of Modern History* 14 (1942): 145-60.

Gilbert, F. "German Historiography during the Second World War." *American Historical Association Review* 53 (1947): 50-58.

Goetz, Walter. "Friedrich Meinecke, Leben und Personlichkeit." *Historische Zeitschrift* 174 (1952): 231-50.

Gollwitzer, Heinz. "Bayern in der Weimarer Republik." *Vierteljahrshefte für Zeitgeschichte* 3 (1955): 365-87.

Gumbel, E. J. "Die Ursacher der politischen Morde." *Das Forum* 9:3 (December 1928).

Hammen, O. J. "German Historians and the Advent of the National Socialist State." *Journal of Modern History* 13:2 (June 1941): 161-88.

Hartshorne, E. Y. "Numerical Changes in the German Student Body: with Editorial Comment." *Nature* 142:133 (23 July 1938): 175-76.

Heller, H. "Universitätsreform." *Neue Rundschau* 42:1 (May 1931): 685-94.

Hertzman, Lewis. "Founding of the German National People's Party. November 1918—January 1919." *Journal of Modern History* 30 (March 1958): 24-36.

Herzfeld, Hans. "Zwei Werke G. Ritters zur Geschichte des Nationalsozialismus und der Widerstandsbewegung." *Historische Zeitschrift* 182 (1956): 321-32.

Hill, Leonidas E. "A New History of Resistance to Hitler." *Central European History* 4 (December 1981): 372-87.

Holborn, Hajo. "Der deutsche Idealismus in sozialgeschichtlicher Beleuchtung." *Historische Zeitschrift* 174 (October 1952): 359-84.

Jacobsen, Hans Adolf. "Kampf um Lebensraum: zur Rolle des Geopolitikers Karl Haushofer im Dritten Reich." *German Studies Review* 4:1 (1981): 79-104.

Kohn, Hans. "Re-thinking Recent German History." *Review of Politics* 14 (1952): 325-45.

Kuhn, Helmut. "Das geistige Gesicht der Weimarer Zeit." *Zeitschrift für Politik* 8 (1961): 1-10.

Laqueur, Walter. "The Role of the Intelligentsia in the Weimar Republic." *Social Research* 39:2 (1972): 213-27.

Mann, Thomas. "The Years of My Life." *Harper's Magazine* (October 1950): 250-68.

Maunz, Theodor. "Hans Nawiasky. Nachruf." *Chronik der Ludwig-Maximilians Universität* (1961-1962): 18.

Nolte, Ernst. "Die deutsche Universität und der Nationalsozialismus." *Neue Politische Literatur* 12 (1967): 236-39.

Paetel, Karl O. "Deutsche im Exil: Randbemerkungen zur Geschichte der politischen Emigration." *Aussenpolitik* 6 (1955): 572-85.

Pross, Harry. "On Thomas Mann's Political Career." *Journal of Contemporary History* 2 (1967): 65-80.

Reinold, Anne-Marie. "Bibliography on Friedrich Meinecke." *Historische Zeitschrift* 174 (1952): 503-23.

Ritter, Gerhard. "German Professors in the Third Reich." *Review of Politics* 8 (April 1946): 242-54.

Rüssel, Herbert. "Max Scheler und die Probleme der deutscher Politik." *Hochland* 27 (April-September 1930): 518-29.

Schieder, Theodor. "Die deutsche Geschichtswissenschaft im Spiegel der *Historischen Zeitschrift*." *Historische Zeitschrift* 189 (1959): 1-72.

Schwabe, Klaus. "Zur politischen Haltung der deutschen Professoren im ersten Weltkrieg." *Historische Zeitschrift* 193 (1961): 601-34.

_____. "Ursprung und Verbreitung des altdeutschen Annexionismus in der deutschen Professorenschaft im Ersten Weltkrieg." *Vierteljahrshefte für Zeitgeschichte* 14:2 (April 1966): 105-58.

Seemann, Ulrich. "Bemerkungen zur Haltung der deutschen Intelligenz gegenüber den Politischen Grundfragen der Deutschen Nation wahrend der Zeit der Weimarer Republik." *Wissenschaftliche Zeitschrift der U. Rostock* 13:4 (1964): 369-94.

Seier, Helmut. "Der Rektor als Führer." *Vierteljahrshefte für Zeitgeschichte* 12 (1964): 105-46.

Sims, Amy. "Intellectuals in Crisis: Historians under Hitler." *Virginia Quarterly Review* 54:2 (1978): 246-62.

Sontheimer, Kurt. "Tatkreis." *Vierteljahrshefte für Zeitgeschichte* 7:3 (July 1959): 229-60.

_____. "Thomas Mann als politischer Schriftsteller." *Vierteljahrshefte für Zeitgeschichte* 6 (1958): 1-44.

Speer, Julius. "Gedenkfeier für die Widerstandskampfer der Universität, 23 February 1961." *Chronik der Ludwig-Maximilians Universität* (1961): 32-37.

Spranger, Eduard. "Mein Konflikt mit der national-sozialistischen Regierung 1933." *Universitas: Zeitschrift für Wissenschaft, Kunst, und Literatur* 10 (1955): 457-74.

Stern, Fritz. "The Political Consequences of the Unpolitical German." *History* 3 (1960): 104-34.

Suval, Stanley. "Overcoming Kleindeutschland: The Politics of Historical Mythmaking in the Weimar Republic." *Central European History* 2 (1969): 312-30.

Szaz, Zoltan Michael. "The Ideological Precursors of National Socialism." *Western Political Quarterly* 16 (1963): 924-45.

Vossler, Karl. "Universität und Bildung." *Bayerland* 37 (1926): 650.

Vossler, Otto. "Humboldt's Idee der Universität." *Historische Zeitschrift* 178 (1954): 251-68.

Wenzl, Aloys. "Erinnerungen aus der Geschichte der Letzten 50 Jahre Unserer Universität." *Jahrbuch der Ludwig-Maximilians Universität 1957-1958*, 53-61.

Wolfson, Philip. "Friedrich Meinecke, 1882-1954." *Journal of the History of Ideas* 17:4 (October 1956): 511-25.

Zeender, John K. "German Catholics and the Concept of an Interconfessional Party, 1900-1922." *Journal of Central European Affairs* 23:4 (January 1964).

_____. Review article. *The Catholic Historical Review* 70:3 (July 1984): 428-41.

Zorn, Wolfgang. "Student Politics in the Weimar Republic." *Journal of Contemporary History* 5:1 (1970): 128-43.

Personal Interviews

Inge Aicher-Scholl, Ulm, January 1972

Dr. Paul Collmer, Stuttgart, January 1972

Theodor Eschenburg, Tübingen, January 1972

Prof. Helmut Hatzfeld, The Catholic University of America, Washington, April 1973

Helmut Heiber, Institut für Zeitgeschichte, November 1971
Prof. Wilhelm Hoffman, Stuttgart, January 1972
Dr. Helmut Krausnik, Institut für Zeitgeschichte, November 1971
Prof. Helmut Kuhn, University of Munich, October 1971
Dr. Otto Lerchenmüller, University of Munich, December 1971
Hans Rothfels, Tübingen, January 1972
Dr. Fritz Ringer, MIT, Summer 1971
Josef Schwarz, Heidelberg, January 1972
Kurt Sontheimer, University of Munich, December 1971
Albert Speer, Heidelberg, January 1972
Dr. Hermann Tüchle, University of Munich, October 1971
Emil Weber, Heidelberg, January 1972

Index